Sex Texts from the Bible

Books in the
SkyLight Illuminations Series

Bhagavad Gita: Annotated & Explained
The Book of Mormon: Selections Annotated & Explained
Dhammapada: Annotated & Explained
The Divine Feminine in Biblical Wisdom Literature: Selections Annotated & Explained
The End of Days: Essential Selections from Apocalyptic Texts—Annotated & Explained
Ethics of the Sages: Pirke Avot*—Annotated & Explained*
Gnostic Writings on the Soul: Annotated & Explained
The Gospel of Philip: Annotated & Explained
The Gospel of Thomas: Annotated & Explained
Hasidic Tales: Annotated & Explained
The Hebrew Prophets: Selections Annotated & Explained
The Hidden Gospel of Matthew: Annotated & Explained
The Lost Sayings of Jesus: Teachings from Ancient Christian, Jewish, Gnostic and Islamic Sources—Annotated & Explained
Native American Stories of the Sacred: Annotated & Explained
Philokalia: The Eastern Christian Spiritual Texts—Annotated & Explained
The Qur'an and Sayings of Prophet Muhammad: Selections Annotated & Explained
Rumi and Islam: Selections from His Stories, Poems, and Discourses—Annotated & Explained
The Sacred Writings of Paul: Selections Annotated & Explained
The Secret Book of John: The Gnostic Gospel—Annotated & Explained
Selections from the Gospel of Sri Ramakrishna: Annotated & Explained
Spiritual Writings on Mary: Annotated & Explained
Tao Te Ching: Annotated & Explained
The Way of a Pilgrim: Annotated & Explained
Zohar: Annotated & Explained

Sex Texts from the Bible

Selections Annotated & Explained

Translation & Annotation
by Teresa J. Hornsby

Foreword by Amy-Jill Levine

Walking Together, Finding the Way
SKYLIGHT PATHS®
PUBLISHING
Woodstock, Vermont

Sex Texts from the Bible:
Selections Annotated & Explained

2007 First Printing

Library of Congress Cataloging-in-Publication Data
Hornsby, Teresa J., 1959–
Sex texts from the Bible : selections annotated & explained / translation & annotation by Teresa J. Hornsby ; foreword by Amy-Jill Levine.
p. cm. — (SkyLight illuminations series)
Includes bibliographical references.
ISBN-13: 978-1-59473-217-1 (quality pbk.)
ISBN-10: 1-59473-217-5 (quality pbk.)
1. Sex—Biblical teaching. 2. Bible—Quotations. I. Title.

BS680.S5H6134 2007
220.8'3067—dc22

2006036151

10 9 8 7 6 5 4 3 2 1

Manufactured in the United States of America
Cover design: Walter C. Bumford III, Stockton, Massachusetts

SkyLight Paths Publishing is creating a place where people of different spiritual traditions come together for challenge and inspiration, a place where we can help each other understand the mystery that lies at the heart of our existence.

SkyLight Paths sees both believers and seekers as a community that increasingly transcends traditional boundaries of religion and denomination—people wanting to learn from each other, *walking together, finding the way*.

Walking Together, Finding the Way®
Published by SkyLight Paths Publishing
A Division of LongHill Partners, Inc.
Sunset Farm Offices, Route 4, P.O. Box 237
Woodstock, VT 05091
Tel: (802) 457-4000 Fax: (802) 457-4004
www.skylightpaths.com

Contents

Destructive Sexuality

Sexual Joy and Delight

Foreword

Amy-Jill Levine

With biblical illiteracy reaching an all-time high and sanctimonious polemic achieving new depths of disgust, finally we have a collection that cuts through the ignorance and odium to explain not only *what* the Bible says about sex, but also *why*. Because it attends to diverse views, historical contexts, and linguistic nuance, this collection disarms the Bible from its crass use in today's culture wars and instead invites you to develop your own interpretations. For this service, Teresa Hornsby deserves the gratitude of all readers of the Bible.

People of good will, theological concern, and personal integrity will find themselves on the opposite sides of many of the issues that fall, directly or elusively, under the rubric of the Bible and sexuality. This does not necessarily mean that one view is right and the other wrong. It *does* mean, however, we should not demonize those whose interpretations differ from our own.

All readers interpret, and interpretation is necessary to make sense of the Bible. For example, we must distinguish between literal injunction and metaphor or hyperbole. Is "if your right hand causes you to sin, cut it off and throw it away" (Matthew 5:30a, part of the Sermon on the Mount) imperative or exaggeration? Is it a condemnation of a particular behavior, such as envy or stealing or masturbation or, less likely although I've heard this one as well, cracking your knuckles?

At times, we decide a text is outdated or contrary to divine will; such is the case with 1 Peter 2:18, "Slaves, accept the authority of your masters with all deference, not only those who are kind and gentle but also those who are harsh." Passages exhorting such obedience are also part of the discussion of the Bible and sexuality, since the slave's body belonged to the master and so could be, and was, used for sexual purposes.

At other times, we ignore the primary meaning. First Timothy 2:15 states that women gain their salvation in child bearing; most churches do not teach this today, or they change the translation to suggest the author is talking about the birth of one particular child, namely, Jesus. No major church today insists that women must procreate in order to be saved. In like manner, Jesus mentions that "You have heard that it was said, 'An eye for an eye and a tooth for a tooth'" (Matthew 5:38, citing Exodus 21:24; Leviticus 24:20; Deuteronomy 19:21). Indeed, the people had, but people at the time did not take the injunction literally. Rather, monetary compensation substituted for physical mutilation.

Once we determine the best meaning of a statement, our need to interpret is not complete. We must ask: Is the statement under discussion addressed to everyone or one group or one person? Is it good for all time, or is it historically and culturally contingent? For example, when the first humans are told, in Genesis 1, "be fruitful and multiply and fill the earth and subdue it," does the commandment hold for men and women both, or just for men (a debate among some ancient Rabbis)? What about overpopulation? What about those who are infertile? Can one be fruitful and multiply through means other than procreation, such as preaching the gospel, or working for organizations like Doctors without Borders? Similarly, when Paul tells women in Corinth that they should remain silent (see 1 Corinthians 14:33b–36), is he speaking only to women in Corinth, or just to married women in Corinth, or to all women everywhere? Why would we, today, in Nashville or New York, be reading mail addressed to a church in Greece?

One way of sorting through diverse texts and diverse interpretations is to find a touchstone of truth. That touchstone might be what the Gospels refer to as the "Greatest Commandment," taken from Deuteronomy 6 and Leviticus 19. Matthew 22:36–40 has an interlocutor ask Jesus: "Teacher, which commandment in the Law is the Greatest?" Jesus responds, "'You shall love the Lord your God with all your heart and with all your soul, and with all your mind.' This is the greatest and first commandment. And the second is like it: 'you shall love your neighbor as yourself.'" For others, the touchstone is the prophet Micah's advice that all the Lord requires is to "do justice, and to love kindness, and to walk humbly with your God" (Micah 6:8). Or that touchstone may be our own hearts and minds, or the teachings of our particular religious tradition.

How then should we read these texts that Teresa Hornsby has assembled? We might follow Matthew's description of the "scribe trained for the kingdom of heaven"—the one who takes out of his "treasure box" (the Greek is *thesaurus*) both what is old and what is new (Matthew 13:52). Look to the past, to the Scriptures, but also look to the future. Do not dismiss history or tradition, science or personal experience. Moreover, theologically speaking, communication between heaven and earth does not stop with the close of the biblical canon. To the contrary, each tradition that holds these texts sacred has a sense of ongoing revelation—through the Holy Spirit, through the teachers of the community, through the communion of the individual reader and the Scriptures. If we restrict our religious understanding to the pages of the Bible, we are engaging in what is called bibliolatry: we have turned the Bible into an idol, rather than allowed it to remain a living text that speaks anew to each generation.

Finally, I suggest that we look at the Bible not as an "answer" book to life's questions. We might see it instead as a question book—a book that raises the seminal (or, if you prefer, ovarial—metaphors do say a lot about us) questions about life, our place in it, and our relationship to that which is greater than our individual selves.

Acknowledgments

Writing this book was a joy. I looked forward to opening these pages each day and writing down all the things I have learned, thought about, and taught during the last decade. I have published many articles and book chapters that were written for other scholars in my field, and I often wondered if anyone ever really read them. And if so, did they matter? This book matters. It encases at least a hundred years of Bible scholarship about passages that have shaped some of our modern attitudes about sex. So, as these are the acknowledgments, I would like to acknowledge two fears.

My first fear is that my academic colleagues will dismiss this book because of its simplicity. I make complicated theories accessible to everyone (it's what I do in my classes every day). I know from my academic training that for every statement I make about historical context, authorial intent, or word meanings, there are at least four valid and sound arguments to the contrary. For this book, I explored the possibilities and chose the one or two that seem most plausible and most supported.

My second fear is that my Ozark neighbors will find the book to be too light, too funny, or too disrespectful. I love the Bible: its history, its stories, and the hope it gives. I am also aware of the damage it can bring. It's like a knife: in the hands of a killer it's a weapon; in the hands of a surgeon it's a lifesaver. I don't want this book to appear to anyone as an attack on the Bible. It is a sincere effort to read the Bible in a way that clarifies and makes relevant and accessible some crucial biblical passages.

I want to thank my students. They are the ones who ask the questions that this book attempts to answer. The students know how important their questions are and that they must be answered. What the Bible has to say about sex matters on a personal level, a national level, and a global level. Historically laws prohibiting certain couplings, for example, interracial marriage, were often biblically based. Today, legislative decisions about gay marriage or about funding sexually related programs, such as abstinence education and international and domestic family planning, often rely heavily on biblically based arguments. My students know this and we talk about it. We talk about it a lot. So, I thank them for making me always think about the intersection of politics, sex, and the Bible. They force me to always keep my work current and relevant.

I also thank my best friends and colleagues, Dr. Regina Waters and Dr. Steve Mullins, for many, many "socially lubricated" yet highly intellectual conversations. I find their feedback on this material invaluable. I have also had the very best Bible professor, critical thinker, and friend as my mentor since 1996—Amy-Jill Levine. Nothing I do could have happened without her.

I have wonderful support from friends and colleagues at Drury University in Springfield, Missouri. I thank Dr. Lisa Esposito and Dr. Charles Taylor for their support of my scholarship. I continue to value my conversations with Dr. Melisa Klimaszewski and I appreciate her exceptional insights, her critical eye, and our shared bizarre sense of humor. Finally, I have so much gratitude for Ruth Arick, to whom I dedicate this book. She is a wise woman who makes everything so much easier. She has given me a most valuable gift: clarity.

Sex and the Bible: Why You Should Care

This book is a culmination of my thoughts about the Bible since I was about seven years old. While church was pretty much my whole social life, it was also intellectually attractive to me. I loved the history and just thinking about who Jesus was and what the world was like then. I remember, though, being surprised when I heard preachers who railed against Jews, homosexuals, and even communists. As a naïve young woman, I didn't even know what those words meant, but it didn't make sense that a book about Jesus, who to me was all about peace and love (I was an aspiring hippie—I'd seen them on television), would be used to encourage hate. This book, then, is an attempt to bridge divisions between biblical authority and us. It is a Bible-based reference for understanding sexual sameness and sexual difference. Like politics and religion, sex and religion also seem unlikely bedfellows. But the language of religion is the language of sex: passion, ecstasy, desire. Both religion and sex derive from the impulses of humanity to merge intimately with God and with one another. The problem is that we tend to vilify and demonize those who "come together" differently than we do.

For example, in May 1970, the Billy Graham Crusade came to Knoxville. As an eleven-year-old growing up in an East Tennessee Southern Baptist rural church, I had never seen anything like it. We went to it every night; my mother sang in the choir. One night, President Nixon spoke. I had no idea who he was—I mean, I knew he was the president, but I didn't know what he represented at the time; my only experience of the Vietnam War was that my mother's beloved brother Rob was killed there in 1966. There were protesters, riot police, guns, crosses, and Bibles everywhere. That was the first time I really saw religion and politics clash.

At the time, I thought, "Why are these people here? This is a worship service." It took years before I could answer that question. Political activism and Christian fundamentalism are not mutually exclusive; both share the same passions about the souls of humanity. Both groups can often intend love but come across as crazed zealots.[1]

Most people I've talked to about the Bible and sex come to the topic with one of three assumptions on their mind: (1) "What the Bible has to say about sex is totally irrelevant; whatever people did and said about sex in some foreign land a bazillion years ago has absolutely nothing to do with me"; (2) "I'm not sure what this has to do with me, but at least it will be great stuff to talk about at parties"; or (3) "This must have something to do with me; people are always quoting the Bible when they talk about sex. I would like to know what that's about." This book has something for each of these groups.

Whether we realize it or not, our attitudes about sex in the United States emerge largely from translations and interpretations of the Bible. When we deliberate the morality of premarital sex, divorce, masturbation, and gay marriage, the current social debates and laws on these topics are founded on the Bible. Now, you might think, like the first group, that whatever the Bible says about anything is completely irrelevant. That approach would be true if you lived on an island all by yourself, or if you had no intention of having a conversation with anyone else ever again. Our sexual concerns and the sexuality of others permeate our everyday existence. Sex is everywhere: it sells cars, it entertains us, it makes us money, and it gives us pleasure. Because sex is ever present in our culture, and because the Bible addresses sex, what the Bible says can't help but be relevant.

The second assumption is that the Bible has a lot of cultural currency. Right now the Bible is definitely "in." In fact, one reason I decided to write this book is because of what I've discovered when I travel and find myself in airports, airplanes, and other public venues. People usually ask what I do. When I tell them that I study the Bible and sex, well, here we go.

There is an enormous amount of curiosity about how these two topics go together. Not only that, but even if you consider yourself to be a religious outsider, the topic has seeped—no, *flooded*—into the public consciousness with the book and film *The Da Vinci Code.* While the Bible and sexuality may have once been interesting points of conversation to some, they have now moved to the center of public consumption. The question, specifically, of whether Jesus had sex has become all-consuming for the American public in general.

It is both surprising and expected that Jesus's sexuality would cause a stir. On the one hand, that so many people would be surprised at the idea of Jesus having sex is strange because the idea of Jesus and Mary Magdalene as lovers has been around for nearly two millennia. Some early Christians portrayed Mary Magdalene as a favorite disciple of Jesus to whom he gave secret teachings. Artists later depicted her as the lover in Song of Songs, searching for her love in the garden. This depiction is an allegory of Christ and his beloved, the church. The earthly church is represented by Mary Magdalene. She (the church) seeks spiritual consummation with Christ, yet the artistic imagery is highly erotic.

On the other hand, the popular preoccupation with Jesus's sexuality is an expected frenzy because we have been conditioned to believe that sex and Christianity (as we have interpreted the Bible, the prophets, the priests, and Jesus) are incompatible. We believe this is true primarily because of how we have been taught. When we look closer at the Bible, at its alternative translations, and at some of the original language, the Bible is not as anti-sex as you might think. And, when it is anti-sex, it is for unexpected reasons, and sometimes for reasons that make no sense to us. All in all, the Bible does have relevant things to say about our own sexuality. And we should know what it says and what it doesn't say, because so much of what we and others do sexually is often judged based on what people think the Bible says.

At the same time, just as we might expect, some (but certainly not all) of the things the Bible has to say about sex seem pretty meaningless to us today. It is surprisingly non-judgmental on topics we think it should be adamant about—for example, visiting prostitutes, having more than one wife at a time, and having sex with your daughter—and it complicates topics we may be indifferent about, like how soon a person can have sex after childbirth.

When we consider sex texts in the Bible, there are two very important differences between then and now. First, women's sexuality was a form of property in ancient Israel. A man owned things such as slaves, animals, and women. In some cases, the more powerful and rich a man was, the more women he owned. Laws about what we would consider sexual violations today, including adultery, premarital sex, and rape, were laws about property crimes in the Bible.

Second, much of what is said about sex in the Bible is allegorical. Many of the prophesies and the narratives include examples of sex, rape, incest, and domestic violence. The Bible describes those situations in exactly the same way it describes the ongoing and sometimes disastrous relationship between God and God's people. For example, if Israel were worshiping other gods, the Bible story would talk about an adulterous woman cheating on her husband. Israel has a marriage covenant with God, so to speak. We find the same theme in the Book of Revelation: Christians are considered adulterers for participating in "pagan" culture. A story of incestuous rape, like Amnon's rape of his sister Tamar (both the offspring of David), foreshadows a civil war that literally tears apart the house of David. So, some of the verses that people read as binding upon our personal lives may have been intended primarily as allegorical commentary on the spiritual state of the Israelites the Israelites and Christians.

Nevertheless, regardless of whether we accept the authority of the Bible or not, the Bible is a principal modern resource on sex. The Bible makes declarative statements about sex, such as "a man who lies with a man as with a woman shall be put to death" (Leviticus 20:13). What do we make of this passage? Do we know what this passage really says and what the words mean? Why would the Israelites want to kill men who have sex with other men while other societies found it acceptable (or at least tolerable)? Are we, as modern Americans, obliged to follow this law even if we are not Israelites? If I believe that the Bible is authoritative for me—that is, the Bible guides me daily in my family life, my business dealings, and my political leanings—I have to grapple with this passage and others like it.

Today, many folks for whom the Bible is a central part of their lives also have close gay friends. How do they balance the commandment to "love your neighbor" with the commandment to kill gay men? Moreover, is there a connection between the hate crimes committed against gay and lesbian people and what the Bible says in Leviticus 20 or what Paul writes in Romans 1? The Bible affects our personal and social sentiments about sexuality; it can encourage in us compassion and acceptance or prejudice and violence. Therefore, being both sexual and ethical people, we must examine those texts. We should at least know what the Bible says about sex because it is used to justify discrimination and even violence toward certain types of sexual behaviors.

The texts I have chosen for this book are thematically grouped. You may want to know what the Bible says about marriage in general, or perhaps your interests are more specific, such as interracial marriage, polygamy, or intergenerational marriage. Some of the texts I have chosen may already be familiar to you: the story of Sodom, or the impregnation of Mary, for example. Others are not so common, such as the story of a woman who drinks a potion that may cause a miscarriage, or the story of a woman whose father-in-law mistakes her for a prostitute. The Bible is full of stories, laws, and teachings about sexuality, though often the sexual encounters and the reasons for intercourse may strike us as odd. For example, a primary reason for having sex in the times of both testaments is to make sure you have an heir so that your possessions stay in your family. For many people today, producing an heir would probably not be in the top five reasons for having sex.

One of the problems with choosing biblical texts for modern sexual topics is that many of our notions are, well, modern. For example, there is no biblical Hebrew or Greek word for "homosexuality." There is no word for "abortion." In fact, in biblical Hebrew, there is no word for "marriage." In these cases, I have chosen texts that ministers, scholars, translators, and interpreters have traditionally used to address these matters. Depending on the passage, I may use several methods of analysis. I may discuss a Hebrew or Greek word that has alternative translations that may radically change the meaning, or at least shift the meaning, of a passage. I may also tell you the historical circumstances behind and within the story, or how the story might have been used in its historical context. Knowing about context and extenuating circumstances brings the passage to life and opens its meanings to us. In every passage I explore the relevance to us today. Sometimes this is a no-brainer, sometimes we'll work harder; yet you will continually see the Bible's teachings about sex in a new and different way.

I have written this book with a particular person in mind: you. If you are a human being interested in sex and slightly (or enormously) curious about what the Bible has to say about sex, this book is written exclusively for you. You may be a student, a clergy member, a parent, or a person who just wants to know what the Bible has to say about sex. This book is a serious, and sometimes slightly irreverent, conversation with you. I am an academic Bible scholar and I teach undergraduates in Springfield, Missouri. I endeavor daily to package information that I think is exciting and relevant so that my students will also find it exciting and relevant. I wrote this book to do the same for you.

Much of the groundbreaking scholarship on these passages has already been written by esteemed scholars in my field (Athalya Brenner, Bernadette Brooten, Claudia Camp, William Countryman, Amy-Jill Levine, Jane Schaberg, and many more)—I stand on the shoulders of giants. My intention is to summarize basic historical, theological, literary, and linguistic ideas about the Bible and synthesize them with modern attitudes about sex in a conversation with you, so that you will see how relevant and helpful it is to know what the Bible has to say about your sex life.

And when you're finished with this book, I encourage you to explore the works listed in the Suggestions for Further Reading section in the back of this book.

Marriage and Family Life

The book is divided into four main sections: Marriage and Family Life, Women's Sexuality, Destructive Sexuality, and Sexual Joy and Delight. First I look at sexual concerns that tend to be more common and a part of most people's daily lives, such as heterosexual marriage, divorce, spousal cheating, birth control, and masturbation. Often the words *ish* (man) and *isha* (woman) are translated into English as husband and wife. In the Bible, when a man "takes" a woman (becomes betrothed and/or has sex with her) they are considered to be married. There is no marriage ceremony per se, though in the story of Jacob and Leah, there is a mention of a seven-day period after Jacob "goes in to Leah" (their consummation; Genesis 29:27–28) that has been considered some sort of wedding celebration. There is evidence of a marriage contract, called a *ketubah* (which is still used in Judaism), as early as the Babylonian exile. Sometimes a marriage, especially of a second or lesser wife, was no more than a presentation of a gift from man to man. Not very romantic.

Though marriage is more often a business deal than a romantic ritual in the Bible, it takes spousal cheating (adultery) very seriously—that is, if the woman is attached to some other man. If a man is married, there doesn't seem to be much concern about his visiting prostitutes or unattached women (widows or older, unmarried women). Technically, adultery is only committed if a betrothed or married woman is involved. The man who has sex with another man's wife, future wife, or a virgin daughter of marrying age is basically a thief. He is taking something that isn't his, and, in the case of the virgin, he reduces her value; she is essentially damaged goods.

If a married woman cheats on her husband, and she and her lover are caught in the act, both she and the man she had sex with should be killed, according to Leviticus 20:10. (There is an allusion to this Levitical code in John 8, when a woman is brought to Jesus for a legal judgment.) I say "should be killed" because it's possible that these laws were only meant to be deterrents; we don't know if the punishment was ever used. Despite this, similar laws still exist on the books in some countries today. For example, in Morocco, article 418 of the penal code states: "Murder, injury, and beating are excusable if they are committed by a husband on his wife as well as the accomplice at the moment in which he surprises them in the act of adultery." And in Jordan: "He who discovers his wife or one of his female relatives committing adultery and kills, wounds, or injures one of them, is exempted from any penalty."[2] These are only two examples of at least ten penal codes along these lines.

Divorce is mentioned a few times in the Bible, though not as often as adultery. It is not clear how easy it is to get a divorce in the Hebrew Bible. Jesus, on the other hand, forbids divorce in Mark, though he allows it for sexual immorality in Matthew.

Birth control and abortion aren't mentioned specifically in the Bible at all. It tells us not to "pass our children through the fire," a possible reference to child sacrifice. Also, there is a mention of a child being left in her birth blood out in an open field, which may be a possible reference to infanticide, but the Bible never explicitly names either abortion or infanticide. There are some passages that we use today to defend or attack abortion, and there may be some allusions to controlling fertility—the use of certain herbs, for example—so I will examine all of these passages to see what they have to say to us.

This section also addresses sexuality we might consider off the beaten path, so to speak, but that is still a part of everyday life for many folks in the United States and elsewhere. For example, the Bible has a lot to say about marrying outside your ethnic group. In modern times, these prohibitions are often used to forbid interracial relationships, though "race" is a misnomer here. Surprisingly, sometimes the Bible is in favor of marrying outside your ethnic group, sometimes not. And even when the Bible is vehemently against marrying foreigners, it isn't for reasons you would suspect. Likewise, the Bible's laws are harsh against homoeroticism, particularly for men. On the other hand, there are hints of love and tenderness between persons of the same sex in both the Hebrew Bible and the New Testament. It forbids cross-dressing but praises eunuchs, castrated men.

On the topics of sexual abstinence, celibacy, and fertility, we again get mixed messages. The authors of the Hebrew Bible see babies as a sign of God's blessings. For the apostle Paul, celibacy was preferable to sex, but if you couldn't help yourself, you should get married and have sex. For the later Christian authors, marriage was ordained by God as a sacrament, and having babies was a way for women to obtain salvation.

Women's Sexuality

The second major section attends to the tricky topic of women's sexuality. I say "tricky" because the Bible's authors were pretty much men writing for men on how to control the sexuality of women. Not only do we get a one-sided, unattractive view of women, it is also extremely difficult to figure out if the Bible is talking about "real" women or just symbols of Israel and the church. Women are depicted as property and their sexuality as polluting, if not downright evil. For the most part, female sexuality works to seduce men away from God. In the Bible, the female sex often stands for the foreign god. The seductress lures young men away from "good" women just as the foreign gods lure the Israelites away from God (her good husband). Topics that deal specifically with women in both the Hebrew Bible and the New Testament are veiled under presumptions of uncleanness, impurity, shame, seduction, treachery, and death.

I discuss women's sexuality within the following contexts: menstruation, abortion, contraception, virginity, and prostitution. The Bible mentions prostitution, virginity, and menstruation specifically, but it only makes vague allusions to abortion and contraception. There are verses and passages that some people read to support or oppose abortion, but neither the word "abortion" nor any explicit description of it appears in the Bible.

At the same time, the Bible has much to say in its laws and narratives about making sure a woman is a virgin until she is married. Virginity is a complex category in the Hebrew Bible because a woman's monetary value and her father's honor are tied up in it. I also discuss the virginity of Jesus's mother, Mary.

Prostitutes appear in the Bible as much as, if not more than, virgins. The Hebrew Bible has a fond place for prostitutes. In a few stories (e.g., Joshua 2) they are the salvation of Israel and the road to monarchy. In other stories they lure young and foolish men down the road to ruin. Oddly enough, the Bible never condemns prostitutes (unless one happens to be a daughter of a priest), nor does it prohibit sexually available men from visiting them on occasion. Prostitutes appear in Solomon's story of wisdom (1 Kings 3:16–27); Jesus is accused of dining with them (Matthew 9:11; Luke 5:30); and Paul warns the Corinthians about the ills of going to prostitutes, which suggests that they must have visited them on occasion (1 Corinthians 6:16).

Destructive Sexuality

The third section of this book addresses destructive sexuality—rape, sexual violence, incest. It also addresses bestiality, which occurs only in legal prohibition. The Bible has strong portrayals of rape. There are incestuous rapes, gang rapes, and laws about rape. However, rape, like adultery, tends to fall under the category of property crime rather than sexual offense. If you have sex with another man's wife or daughter without his consent (or hers, which is what makes it rape rather than adultery), then you are essentially stealing from your neighbor and shaming a woman of the community. Keeping the community whole (and holy) is of paramount importance, as we'll see later in this introduction.

There is an abundance of passages that depict domestic violence, particularly in the Prophets. The problem is, God is usually the abusive husband. Though the New Testament specifically tells husbands not to deal harshly with their wives, it also tells the wives to suffer silently if their husbands do abuse them. There is not much comfort in the Bible for women who are victims of domestic violence.

Depictions of incest in the Bible are problematic for a number of reasons. First, the Bible does not explicitly forbid sex between a father and a daughter in its lists of "you shall nots." Second, the stories of incest tend to be etiological tales, which are tales that give the origins of something. When a father has sex with a daughter, for example, the offspring from that copulation is usually a hated enemy. So, even though the Bible does not prohibit father-daughter sex, it provides a not-so-subtle way to say, "our enemies are incestuous bastards."

Sexual Joy and Delight

The final section of this book is all about sexual pleasure and delight. Just as you might be surprised by some of the Bible's harsh pronouncements about sex or about its silence on important sexual topics, you may be surprised to learn that it also celebrates sexual passion, desire, and tenderness. It is my favorite section of the book.

Sometimes sex is all too explicit in the Bible, sometimes it is implicit. Nevertheless, the Bible is all about human beings and their relation to God and to each other. The Bible talks about the relationship with the Divine through sexual metaphors, and it has much to say about our own sexual relations: with whom we should have sex, with whom we should not have sex, when we should have sex, when we should not have sex, how we should have sex, and how we should not have sex. To see how these passages might impact our lives today, it will be helpful first to explore just what the ancient writers had in mind when they wrote, for example, that Sarah would still have sexual pleasure, even as an old lady (Genesis 18:10–12). Or that Isaac and Rebekah were caught fooling around with each other in such a way that the king knew they were not brother and sister as they had claimed, but indeed married. There are treasures to be found in the passages about sexual pleasure if we take the time to read them closely, look at various word meanings, think about historical context, and open our minds to the possibility that there are, indeed, some sexy things going on in the Bible.

Separateness

As I mentioned earlier, the Bible's reasons for all of these sexual directives are often not at all what we would expect. And sometimes they are precisely for reasons we would expect. Like all great sacred traditions and histories of a people, so much of what the Bible has to say derives from a very particular cultural mind-set. The laws, the ancestral stories, the prophets, and the histories of kings, queens, and wars were told, written, rewritten, and edited with very specific ideas about God, foreigners, men and women, and the intersections between all of them. And, at the center of all of these concerns were sex and food. Here is why: the Israelites were interested in maintaining their own culture—not mixing with foreign things. After all, God had commanded them to "be holy as I am holy"(Leviticus 19:2). The Hebrew word for holy also means "separate"—"be separate as I am separate." Thus mixing becomes a bad thing—literally, an abomination. The word for "mixing," *toevah,* gets translated into English as "abomination." Put all of this together and mixing of things that should not be mixed (cultures, foods, clothes, even genders) becomes forbidden in the Bible.

Now this is where sex comes in. Think of a community—for example, ancient Israel—as a gated city. If you wanted to guard that city and make sure nothing unpleasant enters, you would post a guard at its entryways (doors or windows, for example). As non-nomadic peoples often do, it seems the Israelites imagined their communities as a human body. They posted guards (their laws) at its doors and windows (mouth and genitals). The laws intricately laid out in Leviticus and Deuteronomy are more concerned with what goes into our orifices (sex and food) than with anything else.

When things remain separate from one another, they are in their proper place; they are categorized and contained. In other words, they are civilized. The things that are out of place, out of order, belong to the realm of chaos, in the realm of death, that which cannot be controlled. Keeping things in their proper places is a never-ending endeavor. Things always defy categorization. Nothing ever fits neatly into a tidy box. Maintaining order requires constant and vigilant monitoring. Then, when something is out of place, which inevitably happens, we call it "unclean." Soil in a garden is okay, but soil on your shirt and hands is dirty. Pictures of a man's penis in an anatomy class are okay, but those same pictures posted on the Internet on a pornography site would be called "dirty." Things that defy categorization tend to cause anxiety, sometimes even anger. If you can follow this kind of thinking—that things should be in their proper place, and that unlike things should not be mixed—then you are beginning to think like the authors of the Hebrew Bible.

The dire warnings against mixing unlike things applied to many categories in the Bible, but in this book we're most concerned with sex. Regulating the sex of each person meant making sure that sex was controlled and categorized, and not mixed in the "wrong" ways. An obvious example would be bestiality. Humans should not have sex with nonhuman animals; this is "an abomination," that is, a mixing of unlike things (Leviticus 18:23).

Less apparent is the example of male homoeroticism. You might think, "Wouldn't this be an example of two things that are alike having sex?" Rather, here is how the authors of Leviticus and the apostle Paul would have thought of this: when two men have intercourse, one is penetrating and one is being penetrated. The one who penetrates is a man acting like a man (the active sexual partner). The man who is penetrated is a man acting like a woman (the passive sexual partner). Therefore, the two unlike things that are being mixed are the genders: a male is taking on the actions of a female in the same body. It is, according to Leviticus 20:13, an abomination and, according to Paul, unnatural—again, confusion and mixing.

By having sex with the wrong person, each individual was capable of bringing destruction to the entire community. It only takes one unlocked door. Regulating the sexuality of one individual ensures the survival of the whole people. We don't think like this so much today (well, perhaps some people do), but the idea of *all people as one* was the central frame of reference for the Hebrew people.

We also see this way of thinking in some of Paul's letters to the early Christians. For Paul, the Christians had many of the same difficulties as the Israelites. They had to define their identity over and against all of the other peoples and religions while maintaining order and unity within an ethnically and socially diverse community.

Paul envisioned this burgeoning community as a human body—Jesus's body. In 1 Corinthians 6:15–16, he implores people to carry themselves as if each of them is a body part of Jesus. Imagine the radical shift of perspective: if you have sex with a prostitute, Jesus is having sex with a prostitute. If you have sex with your stepmother, Jesus is having sex with your stepmother. This must have been a highly effective strategy for keeping the community unified while avoiding sexual immorality. The early church also saw sexual activity between appropriate persons as a redeeming act. Paul's method for keeping the Christian communities separate (thus holy) was very much like what we observe not only in the Hebrew Bible but also in the greater Hellenistic landscape: he urged them not to mix (e.g., no sex, no marriage with nonbelievers). He and his Hellenistic, non-Jewish contemporaries, like the authors of Leviticus, saw homoeroticism, including female homoeroticism, as an unnatural mixing of unlike things.

The Gospel writers do not seem to give the idea of separateness the weight that we see in Paul's writings, though I think they certainly lived with the same assumptions about "dirt," purity, and holiness. Unlike the authors of Leviticus and the apostle Paul, the central message for the evangelists wasn't building a cohesive and separate community. Rather, it was giving each community a portrait of Jesus that strengthened it.

Still, the evangelists, especially Matthew, develop larger themes that are usually taken as indicative of sexual behaviors. For example, woven throughout much of the gospels is a theme of "higher righteousness." Most of us are familiar with Jesus's fundamental teaching to "turn the other cheek." Yet there is an added sense that Jesus's ideal is to go beyond the expected "goodness." If society expects equal retaliation (if someone smacks you, you smack him back), you respond with a higher righteousness: you make the striker hit you with his or her left hand. This requires an open-handed rather than a back-handed slap. This may not seem like a big deal to us, but Jesus may be referring to a type of nonviolent response that the Jews used in 39 CE to protest the placement of Caligula's statue in the Jerusalem Temple. This response allowed one to retain his or her dignity without responding with more violence. Sexually speaking, Jesus holds us to higher expectations: if you are not supposed to have sex with someone to whom you're not married, don't even look at or think about that person with desire; if you are supposed to divorce only for a reason of spousal cheating, never divorce; if you are supposed to be celibate for God, you should castrate yourself for God. It is a standard that very few of us can achieve.

So, what does all of this separation, holiness, and higher righteousness have to do with us today? My hopes for this book are multilayered. I hope to demystify the Bible—to show that some of it was written to guide people on how to live their lives every day and how to understand and worship God. At the same time, I hope to find in the Bible remedies (instead of causes) for sexual prejudice and shame. I hope to put its ideas about sex in plain language and to soften some of its harshness concerning sexuality by explaining it. The Bible isn't anti-sex. It honors celibacy, but it also urges us to have lots of babies, and sings the praises of sexual pleasure and desire.

Finally, what I most want readers to get from this book is an understanding that sometimes the Bible's directives about sex are helpful and sometimes they are hurtful. The Bible's contents are not "one size fits all." As modern, intelligent readers, we have to take into consideration the historical context and the underlying theological worldviews of those who wrote the Bible. They are very different from our own. We cannot always presume to be in sync with the attitudes of the Bible's writers. As the apostle Paul wrote, "all things may be permitted to me, but not all things are helpful." The Bible's truths and lessons may not be applicable for all times and all people. If you educate yourself and understand the possible intentions of its writers, then it can be an excellent guide to understanding your own sex life and the sex lives of others. The Bible, as sacred scripture, should be a relief and comfort, not a weapon.

The Role of Euphemisms

When I tell people that my work is about sex in the Bible, they generally respond with something like, "There's sex in the Bible?" And I say, "Well, yes, there is actually a *lot* of sex in the Bible." One reason people don't know that there is sex in the Bible is because it is usually hidden behind euphemisms. The sexual euphemism may be in the original language, or it may be the work of a translator. When we read in Genesis 4:17 that "Cain knew his wife, and she conceived," we can be certain that "Cain knew" is a euphemism for his having sex with her. "To know" is a common euphemism for sexual intercourse in the Bible.

In other instances, we find that it is the English translators who have used a euphemism for an explicit Hebrew or Greek sexual term. For example, Deuteronomy 23:1 contains a Hebrew word for penis: *shopkah*. The King James translation substitutes "privy member," the New Revised Standard Version uses "member," and the New American Standard has "male organ."

Often, however, it isn't clear if the word is explicit in the original language. For example, a very common modern euphemism for genitals is "privates." In Deuteronomy 25:11–12 it says: "If men get into a fight with one another, and the wife of one intervenes to rescue her husband from the grasp of his opponent by reaching out and seizing his *mabush,* you shall cut off her hand; show no pity." The Hebrew word *mabush* does not appear anywhere else in the Bible apart from this one verse. Its literal meaning is "something that promotes shame." So, translating it as "secrets" (KJV) or as "privates" makes sense, although some modern translations are more explicit and have used the word "genitals." Words for genitals are always tricky in translation. Modesty and common courtesy often require that we use a euphemism. However, euphemisms tend to be particularly bound to a specific place and time. When a translator of the Bible has "secrets" for testicles, we have to use our imagination and best guesses.

The Bible can also have a phrase that we might find vulgar to describe something very ordinary. For example, the Bible refers to males as "pissers against the wall" (e.g., 1 Samuel 25:22; 1 Kings 14:10). And the Bible sometimes has idioms that must have been crystal clear to its contemporary audience but we can only guess at their meanings. For example, Jeremiah 3:3 charges that "you have the forehead of a whore and refuse to be ashamed." I scratch my head and admit that this idiom is lost to us. We can only guess at what the prophet Jeremiah was thinking when he said that someone has the forehead of a whore.

To begin my commentary on the rich collection of sexual passages in the Bible, I will give some specific examples of some of the common sexual euphemisms in the Bible, including literal, linguistic euphemisms as well as "suggestive" ones. Suggestive passages provide clues to the sex even if there isn't an actual word to point to it; like characters in a movie who wake up in bed together—we didn't see it, but we know what happened last night. This list of euphemisms is not intended to be exhaustive. I just want you to see how a biblical passage may be fraught with sex and you might never see it. Euphemism works like camouflage. The sexual subjects are all around us; we just have to be able to differentiate them from their surroundings.

A Note on the Translation

My starting point and default for each translation was the New Revised Standard Version (NRSV) of the Bible. While my translations follow the NRSV for background material and translations of benign phrases (e.g., descriptions of time and place), I focused on each word that was relevant to the discussion—particularly words suggesting or discounting sexual content, and words that could impact the meaning of the whole passage. For these key words, I went to the Hebrew and Greek manuscripts and lexicons (depending on the passage) to see how the word was used throughout the Bible and in its contemporary literature. I then consulted word studies and current scholarship on unknown, contested, or problematic phrases. I also compared texts to manuscript variations (e.g., if there are several known variations of the same passage) and to other English translations, primarily the King James Version (KJV). Finally, I translated the primary words of each passage myself, based on all I had read and ultimately on what I decided would be most appropriate for the content of the entire section. Sometimes my translation decision was aligned with the NRSV; often it was not.

For example, in the NRSV, Genesis 34:2 has, "He seized her and lay with her by force." The KJV reads, "He took her, and lay with her, and defiled her." I translated this section as, "He took her and lay with her and humiliated her." The crucial word in this sentence is *anah*. The NRSV translates it as "by force." Though it is certainly a possible description of what happened, "by force" is not a common translation of the Hebrew *anah,* which appears in the Bible some eighty-four times. The KJV translates this word as "defiled her," which is also a probable sentiment but introduces the idea of purity (unnecessarily) into the passage. My translation follows the Hebrew as literally as possible. I chose "humiliated" because it captures the sentiment implied by *anah*; it is consistent with the idea of shame and defilement alluded to in the KJV; and my translation is in line with other passages that use the word to show shame and humiliation (see Genesis 31:50 and Deuteronomy 21:14).

Marriage and Family Life

1 The verbs "to go into" and "to enter" are the most common euphemisms for sexual intercourse in the Hebrew Bible. The individual human body was a symbol for the whole community. The genitals were the community's doors and windows. When a man penetrates a woman, he is literally entering her and figuratively coming into the community.

✦ The language is a pun. As Hagar becomes heavier from her pregnancy, Sarah becomes comparatively lighter, both physically and metaphorically.

2 "Lying with" is another extremely common sexual euphemism for sex in the Bible, much like our modern "sleeping with." Rather than saying we're having sex with someone, we usually say we're sleeping with that person.

3 In herbal medicine, often an herb affects the part of the body it most resembles. Mandrakes look like an erect penis, and they were used as aphrodisiacs and fertility drugs. So sometimes just mentioning something like mandrakes or pomegranates (which resemble a vagina and womb) may suggest that there is more sex than meets the eye in the passage.

☐ Euphemisms for Sex and Genitals

Went Into

He went in[1] to Hagar, and she conceived; and when she saw that she had conceived, her mistress became light in her eyes.

—GENESIS 16:4

Then Judah said to Onan, "Go in to your brother's wife and perform the duty of a brother-in-law to her; raise up offspring for your brother."

—GENESIS 38:8

Lie With

Come, let us make our father drink wine, and we will lie with[2] him, so that we may preserve offspring through our father.

—GENESIS 19:32

But she said to her, "Is it a small matter that you have taken away my husband? Would you take away my son's mandrakes also?" Rachel said, "Then he may lie with you tonight for your son's mandrakes."[3]

—GENESIS 30:15

4 This section of Leviticus outlines all of the incest laws. Rather than saying, "do not have sex with your mother," it relies on the euphemism "do not uncover the genitals [often translated as "do not uncover the nakedness"] of your mother."

5 When we think of the story of Ruth and Boaz, we imagine a mighty and tender love; we tend to think of it as the romantic story of an older, handsome, wealthy man taking care of the beautiful and loyal Ruth. Yet sexual encounters in these times were often what we might call "quick and dirty." The man and woman were most likely not naked. He would mount a woman by lifting his garment and covering her with the outer cloak.

6 Ruth is looking for the next of kin to her late husband. This is the levirate custom (see Genesis 38) so that she can produce a legitimate heir.

7 "At the age for love" probably means puberty—she is around twelve or thirteen.

8 This is one of the sections in Ezekiel in which God is the husband and Jerusalem is the wife. This particular example is intensely erotic. The covenant is made in part by sexual intercourse. For Israel and God to have a covenant and to become married, there must be sexual intercourse. "Covering nakedness" is another euphemism for sex and genitals.

9 God "entered" the woman Jerusalem and therefore they have a covenant. The covenant, like all marriages, must be consummated. After the consummation, the groom possesses the bride.

10 Perhaps the servants remember their king as the man who lusted after Bathsheba, the young man who was loved by Jonathan, and the king who has countless wives. In any case, they figure that a beautiful young virgin is just what the king needs to heat him up.

Uncovering Genitals/Nakedness

Do not uncover the genitals of your father, or the genitals of your mother: she is your mother; do not expose her genitals.[4]

—LEVITICUS 18:7

Spread the Cloak/Skirt Over

He said, "Who are you?" And she answered, "I am Ruth, your servant; spread your cloak over your servant,[5] for you are next-of-kin."[6]

—RUTH 3:9

I passed by you again and looked on you; you were at the age for love.[7] I spread the edge of my cloak over you, and covered your nakedness:[8] I pledged myself to you and entered into a covenant with you, says the Lord God, and you became mine.[9]

—EZEKIEL 16:8

To Know

Now King David was old and sickly and they covered him with lots of blankets but he still couldn't get warm. Then, his servants said, "Let's find a young virgin for you.[10] Make her stand in front of you and she will lust for you. She will lie with you and you will get warm." So they searched for a beautiful girl throughout all the territory of Israel, and found

(continued on page 7)

11 You would think that out of all of David's harem of wives they could find someone who would tickle his fancy. Perhaps this is a slander on Israel's women: there were no virgins among them so the servants had to find a foreign woman.

12 Alas, the plan does not work. King David is not the virile young stud anymore. He simply cannot sexually function, or he has lost all interest.

13 Thigh and foot are often euphemisms for genitals in the ancient world. There are several examples in the Bible of having someone make an oath by placing his hand under a man's genitals. This makes sense if you consider the power and respect that the most powerful and respected man's penis and testicles must generate. This is the source of all his power: the future generations, the progeny of his worth. A person swears on his or her most powerful and sacred object. In American courts, we swear on the Bible. Some movie heroes swear on the grave of their father. For Abraham, the most sacred object is his genitals.

14 Abraham was adamant that Isaac, his son, not marry a foreign woman. He sends his servant to Haran so that Isaac can marry a family relative, perhaps to maintain the lines of inheritance.

15 Israel, a.k.a. Jacob, asks his son Joseph to swear an oath. Just as Abraham does in Genesis 24:2–3, he asks Joseph to place his hand under his testicles or penis. For us today, this would be one of the most awkward father-son moments imaginable. By contrast, the son of Solomon, Rehoboam, derides the small size of his father's penis (1 Kings 12:10).

16 Just as Abraham doesn't want Isaac to marry a foreigner, Jacob (Israel) does not want to be buried in a foreign land. The examples are set by the ancestors: remain separate from foreigners in life and in death.

Abishag the Shunammite, and brought her to the king.[11] The girl was very beautiful. She became the king's attendant and served him, but the king did not know her[12] sexually.

—1 KINGS 1:1–4

Feet and Thighs for Genitals

Abraham said to his servant, the oldest of his house, who had charge of all that he had, "Put your hand under my thigh and I will make you swear by the Lord, the God of heaven and earth,[13] that you will not get a wife for my son from the daughters of the Canaanites, among whom I live."[14]

—GENESIS 24:2–3

When the time of Israel's death drew near, he called his son Joseph and said to him, "If I have found favor with you, put your hand under my thigh and promise to deal loyally and truly with me.[15] Do not bury me in Egypt."[16]

—GENESIS 47:29

(continued on page 9)

17 On Naomi's (Ruth's mother-in-law's) advice, Ruth gets herself all dolled up and smelling good and goes down to the threshing floor to hide and wait for Boaz. She deliberately waits until he has finished eating and is a little drunk.

18 She comes out from hiding and stealthily uncovers his "feet." Bible scholar Amy-Jill Levine makes a strong case that Ruth seduces Boaz here. She hides until the time is right, approaches him when he has reclined and is a little tipsy, exposes his genitals, and then lies back and waits for him.

19 This is a rare and odd euphemism that isn't clear to translators. Some interpret "covering his feet" as urinating while others think he could be masturbating, defecating, or having sex with someone.

When Boaz had eaten and drunk, and he was in a pleasant mood, he went to lie down at the end of the heap of grain.[17] Then [Ruth] came quietly and uncovered his feet, and lay down.[18]

—Ruth 3:7

After he had gone, the servants came. When they saw that the doors of the roof-chamber were locked, they thought, "He must be covering his feet in the cool chamber."[19]

—Judges 3:24

✦ The title of this section is in quotation marks because there isn't any dating in the Bible. Fathers agreed that their children would marry; we have no record of courtship rituals in the Bible. This still happens today even in the United States. There is an excellent description of love, betrothal, and marriage in Khaled Hosseini's novel, *The Kite Runner.* The protagonist, Amir, sees a woman and falls in love; he asks his father to arrange a marriage through the young woman's father. After a suitable length of engagement, they are married and kiss for the first time.

1 Abraham had sent his servant to Mesopotamia (to Haran) to find a wife for his son Isaac—he didn't want him to marry a Canaanite woman. Usually a marriage would have been arranged among kin, but since Abraham lived in a foreign land and only with his immediate family and with servants, he sent his most loyal servant to find a wife for Isaac.

2 A tried and true place for a guy to meet girls in the ancient world is the well. The Bible tells us that all the young women (unmarried, most likely) came out around noon daily to fetch water. If you were a guy looking for a girl to marry, you would head to the "old watering hole" (just like our modern singles bar) and pick one out.

✦ When you want to find a suitable partner, go to where they are.

□ "Dating"

I am standing here by the spring of water, and the daughters of the townspeople are coming out to draw water.[1] Let the girl to whom I shall say, "Please offer your jar that I may drink," and who shall say, "Drink, and I will water your camels"—let her be the one whom you have appointed for your servant Isaac. By this I shall know that you have shown steadfast love to my master.[2]

—GENESIS 24:13–14

3 Again, we have an example of a young man who finds his love at a well. In this instance, the shepherds are all gathered there to give their sheep water.

4 The mention of Haran, Laban, and a well should remind all readers that Rebekah, Isaac's wife, was found at a well. Laban is Rebekah's brother. This may indeed be the same well. Later, we'll see it mentioned again and it is referred to as "Jacob's well."

5 Jacob meets the love of his life, Rachel, here. As readers, we should have expected it. The well and water imagery suggests lush fertility, and we already know from Genesis 24:13 that the well is a place where men meet their future wives.

6 It seems unusual that Rachel cares for the sheep, especially as a young girl among the shepherds. This suggests that she has no brother, or that her brothers are doing more important things. Taking the sheep for water was not a difficult job, but it is odd for Rachel, who is perhaps between ten and fifteen years old, though we don't know her age for a certainty. I suspect that she has been sent to the well entirely for the purpose of meeting a potential husband. She would have become betrothed at a young age, in order to marry when she reached puberty.

7 In case you missed it the other three times it is mentioned, Rachel is the daughter of Jacob's mother's brother Laban. In other words, this detail is important. It mostly serves to remind you that this is the place where Rebekah was found for Isaac, but it also is a reminder that Rachel is of Abraham's family.

8 Jacob, with a great burst of strength, removes the stone that covers the well and is able to water Laban's flock. This could be taken as erotic imagery that foreshadows Jacob's sexual prowess yet to come. He symbolically removes any barrier to Laban's "well" (Rachel) and later is able to water (impregnate) his whole flock (Leah, Rachel, Bilhah, and Zilpah) (Genesis 30–31).

As he looked, he saw a well in the field and three flocks of
sheep lying there beside it; for out of that well the flocks were
watered. The stone on the well's mouth was large, and when all
the flocks were gathered there, the shepherds would roll the
stone from the mouth of the well, and water the sheep, and put
the stone back in its place on the mouth of the well.[3] Jacob said
to them, "My brothers, where do you come from?" They said,
"We are from Haran." He said to them, "Do you know Laban
son of Nahor?"[4] They said, "We do." He said to them, "Is it well
with him?" "Yes," they replied, "and here is his daughter Rachel,
coming with the sheep."[5] ... While he was still speaking with
them, Rachel came with her father's sheep; for she kept them.[6]
Now when Jacob saw Rachel, the daughter of his mother's
brother Laban, and the sheep of his mother's brother Laban,[7]
Jacob went up and rolled the stone from the well's mouth, and
watered the flock of his mother's brother Laban.[8]

—GENESIS 29:2–6, 9–10

9 Moses doesn't go to the well to meet a woman, like Abraham's servant, but …

10 … Moses, like Isaac and Jacob, meets his wife at a well. The well as their meeting place makes sense because there was apparently no other place you could meet a woman who wasn't your close relative or a servant. This passage is also a good example of how marriage, in many instances in the Bible, is more likely a political or business transaction than it is a religious or romantic institution.

✦ There is no example of marriage as a sacred ritual in the Bible. "Marriage as sacrament" is a fairly modern religious concept and often works to exclude some groups of people from marrying (persons of different races and different ethnicities, and persons of the same sex).

11 Around noon at Jacob's well: if you were one of John's contemporaries you would perk up your ears. You know from the scriptures that men meet women at a well especially around noon, as Genesis tells us, when the young women come out to fetch water. The subtleties of the introduction to this story would make a reader who is familiar with the Hebrew Bible expect an interaction with a woman, and sure enough, there is one. The author isn't trying to get you to think that Jesus and the Samaritan woman have marital intentions. Rather, it is a narrative method to make the reader think one thing is going to happen and then be surprised by the turn of events. Perhaps the woman herself thinks Jesus is looking for love. He surprises her with talk of "living water," a sexual image that is reframed by John in the context of spiritual love rather than physical love.

✦ There's nothing wrong with going somewhere that will increase your odds of finding a partner (singles bars, bowling allies, church, or sporting events). We're pretty fortunate in this modern age of Internet dating: we don't have to travel far away, like Jacob, to find a partner; we don't have to sit at a well under the noon sun; and we don't have to have our father's permission. On the other hand, face-to-face contact, new love, and parental approval are treasured experiences.

But Moses fled from Pharaoh. He settled in the land of Midian, and sat down by a well.[9] The priest of Midian had seven daughters. They came to draw water, and filled the troughs to water their father's flock. But some shepherds came and drove them away. Moses got up and came to their defense and watered their flock. When they returned to their father Reuel, he said, "Why are you back so soon today?" They said, "An Egyptian helped us against the shepherds; he even drew water for us and watered the flock." He said to his daughters, "Where is he? Why did you leave the man? Invite him to eat." Moses agreed to stay with the man, and he gave Moses his daughter Zipporah in marriage.[10]

—EXODUS 2:15–21

So [Jesus] came to a Samaritan city called Sychar, near the plot of ground that Jacob had given to his son Joseph. Jacob's well was there, and Jesus, tired out by his travels, was sitting by the well. It was about noon.[11]

—JOHN 4:5–6

1 The Hebrew here is interesting—it is plural. If fact, every reference to God in the Bible's first account of the creation of the world is plural (Gods, we, us). However, the corresponding verbs are masculine singular, indicating that *Elohim* (literally, "gods") in context is intended to be read in the singular.

2 Human beings are divinely ordained to have sex with one another. God tells the first human beings to have sex, have lots of it, and make lots and lots of babies.

3 This translation is nothing like what you have read in your Bible, but it follows the Hebrew precisely. The implications of this translation are vast: God creates the *adam*—literally, the androgynous thing from the red earth—and finds that its being alone is not good.

4 One traditional reading of Eve's creation is that she is Adam's helper, or that she is an attempt at improving Adam. A better interpretation is that having two is better than one. It is an affirmation of being in a couple and having a family. And, because Eve is a woman, it is an affirmation of making babies.

5 The first time there are distinct genders in the Bible is in this passage. First, there is only the *adam* (the androgyne taken out of the earth). God pulls a woman (*isha*) out of the *adam* and then the *adam* becomes a male (*ish*).

6 Now that they are separate genders, a man's destiny is to leave his mother and father and become one flesh (again) with the woman. There isn't the command to have babies, just an affirmation that men and women should have sex. The implication for us is that sex is okay, sex is our charge, and sex isn't dirty.

✦ If it is not good for the *adam* to be alone, and if it is supposed to find its own suitable mate, perhaps today we should allow each individual to find his or her own suitable mate.

▢ Marriage

And the Lord[1] blessed them, and the Lord said to them, "Be fruitful and multiply,[2] and fill the earth and dominate it; and rule over the fish of the sea and over the birds of the air and over every living thing that moves upon the earth."

—Genesis 1:28

Then the Lord said, "It is not good that the earth thing is alone;[3] I will for him make a helper."[4]

—Genesis 2:18

Therefore a man[5] leaves his father and his mother and clings to his woman,[6] and they become one flesh.

—Genesis 2:24

7 Sarah's laughter here is a pun. God asks her why she laughed when he told her she would be pregnant soon. Then God tells her that she must call her son Isaac, which means "laughter" in Hebrew.

8 Sarah thinks of being sexually active and fertile as pleasurable and delightful, even as an aged married lady.

9 1 Timothy 3:2 is an excellent example of the importance to the early church of a stable marriage, especially as a foundation for church stability. The bishop should be a married male. The author of Timothy believes that monogamous marriage was the thing that distinguished the orthodoxy (those of the "right doctrine") from "heretical" Christian teachings and from the sexual attitudes of the greater Roman society, which, for example, tolerated having mistresses and homoerotic relationships. In some Christian traditions, this verse has been understood to mean that any man who has been divorced and remarried is not fit for ministry.

✦ We can never stress enough the value of a stable family life. The early Christians based the makeup of the ideal family (husband, wife, children) on a model that made them distinct from the greater Roman culture around them. In some Roman families, the elite males would have a mistress or a younger male lover. Today, we know that loving families come in many varieties. Having two loving and good parents is certainly the best scenario, but it sometimes doesn't work out that way. Having a father and mother in a household simply for the sake of having a "nuclear family" or having the appearance of a "normal family" can often be the worst thing for a child. Some of the best, most nurturing families I know look nothing like the family that 1 Timothy describes.

✦ The catholic Epistles of the New Testament (i.e., those letters written after the time of Paul to the universal [catholic] church) attempt, like Paul, to unify the Christian believers. However, the focus broadened toward drawing boundaries within the Christian communities between "true" Christianity and "heretical" teachings. The teachings of the Deutero-Pauline letters (letters attributed to Paul but probably

(continued on page 20)

So Sarah laughed[7] to herself, saying, "After I have grown old, and my master is old, shall I have pleasure?"[8]

—GENESIS 18:12

Now a bishop must be blameless, a male with one woman modest, sensible, dignified, hospitable, a qualified teacher.[9]

—1 TIMOTHY 3:2

written by his followers after his death) try to provide a long-term blueprint for a thriving church throughout the Roman Empire. Community hierarchy is a primary topic in these epistles; the cornerstone of a strong community is a strong marriage and a sound family life. The writers are writing instructional manuals for everyday living, but at the same time they are writing to correct "heretical" doctrines of celibacy and other forms of asceticism practiced by competing Christianities. Marriage becomes one of the sticky issues. On the one hand, Paul had written that marriage wouldn't be his first choice (he would choose celibacy). On the other hand, Christians who have been labeled "heretical" are also teaching against marriage in favor of celibacy. The author of 1 Timothy encourages marriage as a Christian foundation and lumps celibacy in with demonic teachings. I'm not sure that Paul would approve.

10 The author of 1 Timothy begins with a warning about how some Christians will be lured away from their faith by demonic teachings, that is, teachings that are different from what the author believes.

11 These demonic teachings include a ban on marriage (therefore, celibacy) and abstaining from eating certain foods. Though Jesus, as far as we know, never married, and his disciples were either not married or had abandoned their families, the early church architects were insistent that marriage is the foundation of a true Christianity. This mandate to marry was probably more about cultural conformity than it was about spiritual enlightenment.

✦ In general, Paul is a good model to follow: marriage isn't for everyone and one shouldn't get married simply to fit in.

Now the Spirit expressly says that in later times some will depart from the faith by giving credence to wandering spirits and the teachings of demons.[10] Through the pretensions of liars whose consciences are branded, who forbid marriage and enjoin abstinence from foods which God created to be received with thanksgiving by those who believe and know the truth.[11]

—1 TIMOTHY 4:1–3

12 The writer of this letter expects a woman to marry, even if it is a second marriage (we should assume that the woman's husband died before she has had any children), and to rule her household. She should behave, then, in such a manner so as not to bring attention, shame, or derision from those not within this Christian community. This passage suggests that ruling the household was a normal thing for a woman to do in the second-century Greco-Roman world and, perhaps, was something that other Christian groups did not practice. Rather than assuming that women had lesser roles in those churches deemed "heretical," I would argue that those other Christianities offered women a larger role in the public sphere, including roles in worship, and did not relegate their activity to private spaces. The early Christian orthodoxy sought to set up a model—one in which women would marry, produce heirs for the man, behave properly, and run the household—that was in direct contrast to the "heretical" Christian groups, in which women would teach, prophesy, not marry, not have children, and not be relegated to the house. Marriage, then, was in part a symbol of the social legitimacy of Christian faith. Being single would suggest that you were not a good Christian.

13 Not to marry and bear children was indicative of religious heresy and social deviance. Society still judges and pressures women and men today who choose not to marry or have children. Though women have much more freedom about this than in the early twentieth century, people are suspicious of women who reject a "normal" social life. A woman or man who chooses career over family may have to continually fight the battle with her or his family at each holiday gathering.

✦ The Epistles don't offer much support for men and women who choose not to marry. The better models are found in the Gospels, where Jesus and his disciples (both men and women) focus more on their work than on familial concerns, and in the letters of Paul, who would choose the single life (and did, as far as we know) over marriage.

So I would have younger widows marry, bear children, rule their households,[12] and give the opposition no occasion to revile us.[13]

—1 TIMOTHY 5:14

1 There is no separate word for "husband," "wife," or "marriage" in Hebrew apart from *ish* (man) and *isha* (woman). After the man acquires the woman as his wife, he becomes her *ba'al,* or master. This is the word you will see translated as "husband" in the Hebrew Bible.

2 To divorce a wife, a man only needs to find disfavor with her and charge her with unspecified "lewdness." The Hebrew word here suggests some type of sexual behavior, but it's not a direct accusation of adultery. It's more vague and could include something like exposing too much flesh in public, or maybe even flirting. It appears to be extremely easy to get divorced, though we do not know for certain.

3 This is more than likely a hypothetical situation. Many of the laws probably describe events that never happened. They were likely "what ifs" that worked both to prevent transgressions and to make sure everyone knew the foundations of a "good" community.

4 The whole point of this passage is that once a man divorces a woman, he cannot remarry her. Perhaps the law was in place to prevent men from divorcing their wives on an impulse.

5 One of the possible reasons that a man cannot remarry a woman he has divorced is not relevant to us today. Much of Mosaic Law is about staying separate from other cultures and doing everything possible not to lose the land that God gave them by risking illegitimate or unclear heirs. When clear lines of inheritance are interrupted, the land and its ownership are threatened. The woman has mixed with more than one man, thus has become "unclean." If she becomes pregnant and has been with the two men at three different times (original husband, new husband, original husband again), the line of inheritance is confusing and the land becomes vulnerable.

Divorce

When a man takes a woman and possesses her,[1] if then she finds no favor in his eyes because he has found some lewdness in her,[2] and he writes her a bill of divorce and puts it in her hand and sends her out of his house, and she leaves his house, and if she goes and becomes another man's woman, and the latter master dislikes her and writes her a bill of divorce and puts it in her hand and sends her out of his house,[3] or if the latter husband dies, who took her to be his wife, then her former husband, who sent her away, may not take her again to be his wife,[4] after she has been made unclean; for that is confusion before the Lord, and you shall not bring guilt upon the land which the Lord your God gives you for an inheritance.[5]

—DEUTERONOMY 24:1–4

6 By this time in Jesus's ministry, he is considered a great healer and an authoritative teacher. Matthew tells us that multitudes have followed him from the Galilee into Judea beyond the Jordan, which would be about eighty miles.

7 The Pharisees test Jesus. This isn't antagonistic; it is a legitimate rabbinic style: pose a familiar problem, quote scripture, cite prior rulings. The question is, for what cause can a woman be released from her contract of marriage?

8 Jesus does what any good rabbi would do: he quotes scripture and then adds his own ruling: what God has put together, no human can separate. But what about Moses's ruling in Deuteronomy 24:1, which states that if a man is displeased with a woman because he "finds some lewdness in her," he can divorce her? Jesus counters with a radical ruling: the contract of marriage is one ratified by God and cannot be dissolved for any reason other than sexual misconduct. Matthew argues that Moses allowed divorce only because the people were not ready for the kind of everlasting love and forgiveness that Jesus is teaching. In the ideal world of God's kingdom, marriage is forever.

9 The disciples question Jesus on whether it is practical for a man to marry at all. Jesus restates that not everyone is capable of living his or her life as one would in the kingdom of heaven. The law provides a way to live as close as we can to the teachings of Jesus if we are not able to accept fully the radical teachings of the kingdom.

10 Jesus chooses the example of eunuchs because the state is a permanent one (unlike ascetic celibacy). Jesus's example is of some who permanently sacrifice reproductive intercourse. This is the radical life of the kingdom, which isn't for everyone. Whether you choose to marry or you choose to live life without sex, your choice should be permanent. There is no waffling in the kingdom of heaven.

Now when Jesus had finished these sayings, he went away from Galilee and entered the region of Judea beyond the Jordan; and large crowds followed him, and he healed them there.[6] And Pharisees came up to him and tested him by asking, "Is it lawful to divorce one's wife for any cause?"[7] He answered, "Have you not read that he who made them from the beginning made them male and female, and said, 'For this reason a man shall leave his father and mother and be joined to his wife, and the two shall become one flesh'? So they are no longer two but one flesh. What therefore God has joined together, let no person separate." They said to him, "Why then did Moses command one to give a certificate of divorce, and release her?"[7] He said to them, "For your hardness of heart Moses allowed you to divorce your wives, but from the beginning it was not so. And I say to you: whoever divorces his wife, except for sexual perversions, and marries another, commits adultery."[8] The disciples said to him, "If this is the case of a man with his wife, it is not practical [useful] to marry." But he said to them, "Not all men can receive this saying, but only those to whom it is given.[9] For there are eunuchs who have been so from birth, and there are eunuchs who have been made eunuchs by men, and there are eunuchs who have made themselves eunuchs for the sake of the kingdom of heaven. He who is able to receive this, let him receive it."[10]

—MATTHEW 19:1–12

11 Mark doesn't mention Jesus's healing here as Matthew does. This indicates that in this instance, it is what Jesus is saying that is important—not what he is doing.

12 In Matthew, which was probably written after and dependent on Mark, Jesus first cites God's actions in Genesis and then cites the law of Moses. In Mark, Jesus first invokes Torah and then illuminates it through the act of creation. Again, Jesus's style of arguing Torah is right in line with rabbinical schools of thought.

✦ Mark does not include the radical teaching about the eunuchs, but his teaching that marriage is forever, no matter what, is also pretty shocking. This is the point on which the disciples later question him. Again, Jesus is making the point that a covenant is lasting—there are no loopholes. Matthew drives this point home with an example about being a eunuch; no take-backs indeed! The author of Matthew added the exception of sexual excess (*porneia*) because he did not fully accept or find necessary the radical vision of Jesus's kingdom of God. For Mark, the imminent transformation of the world was at hand—divorce was not a major concern for a community that expected Jesus to appear at any moment. For Matthew, a more realistic model of marriage, one that fits a long time span, must include a way out in the case of sexual immorality (*porneia*). Jesus's teaching on divorce is simple, though some of us may think that it is nearly impossible. God holds us to an extremely high standard: if you marry, it's forever.

He left that place and went to the region of Judea beyond the Jordan and crowds again gathered around him; and, as was his habit, he again taught them.[11] Some Pharisees came, and to test him they asked, "Is it lawful for a man to divorce his wife?" He answered them, "What did Moses command you?" They said, "Moses allowed a man to write a certificate of dismissal and to divorce her." But Jesus said to them, "Because of your indifference he wrote this commandment for you. But from the beginning of creation, 'God made them male and female.'" "For this reason a man shall leave his father and mother and be joined to his wife, and the two shall become one flesh." So they are no longer two, but one flesh. Therefore what God has joined together, let no one separate.[12]

—MARK 10:1–9

✦ In the ancient world, women and their sexuality were property, at least, that is how they have been described in the Bible. The crime of adultery would be an offense against your property—a theft if the woman is older, and theft with property damage if the woman is a virgin. It is difficult for us to think in these terms today. In the Bible, a man's woman is a part of his honor, which is often tied up with his possessions. A woman who participates in adultery brings shame to her owner and to herself. Though the mind-set about what adultery means and the damage it causes is different in the Bible than it is today, it is still something that usually causes a lot of hurt. It remains one of the only noncontested causes for divorce in our laws. But for us, rather than a property crime (though it still can be), it is often a betrayal, a breaking of a promise, and pure evidence for a loss of love. It's a sad event. Even though these writings come to us from fundamentally different worldviews and radically alien cultures, there is still wisdom in some of the words.

1 The narrator is none too pleased with David either as a king or as a man of God. It is spring and David is not where he should be: in battle.

2 David awakens from sleeping in the late afternoon, walks out onto his roof, and spies a beautiful woman bathing. In response to David's question regarding her identity, the woman is acknowledged in the way typical of ancient Israel: by her father and by her husband. This information is important in two ways for the reader: by her father we know that she may not be an Israelite, and by her husband we know that she is another man's property. David sends his men to bring her to him. Perhaps he thinks that as its king, he has full access to all of Jerusalem's possessions.

3 Bathsheba comes with the men to David, but I doubt she has a choice. The king sends his "associates" to fetch a thing he desires; perhaps they stand there while she readies herself; it seems unlikey that his summoning of her is an invitation that warrants an answer, though she may have given her consent. David has sex with her and then sends her home. There is no mention of love, of romance, or of any expectation of future contact.

□ Cheating on Your Spouse

If a man commits adultery with the wife of his neighbor, both the adulterer and the adulteress shall be put to death.

—LEVITICUS 20:10

You shall not commit adultery.

—EXODUS 20:14

Neither shall you commit adultery.

—DEUTERONOMY 5:18

In the spring of the year, the time when kings go to battle, David sent Jo'ab, and his servants with him, and all Israel; and they ravaged the Ammonites, and besieged Rabbah. But David remained at Jerusalem.[1] It happened, late one afternoon, when David arose from sleeping and was walking upon the roof of the king's house, that he saw from the roof a woman bathing; and the woman was very beautiful. And David sent and inquired about the woman. And one said, "Is not this Bathshe'ba, the daughter of Eli'am, the wife of Uri'ah the Hittite?"[2] So David sent messengers, and took her [fetched, snatched]; and she came to him, and he lay with her.[3] (Now she was purifying herself from her uncleanness.) Then she returned to her

(continued on page 33)

4 The narrator is especially concerned that we know she is in some state of purity, which is a curious notion if Bathsheba isn't an Israelite. Uncleanness of women in the scriptures refers to either menstruation or childbirth. In either case, if Bathsheba's bath was a purification ritual, the important detail here is that Bathsheba has been menstruating or has just delivered a child. In other words, Bathsheba is not (yet) pregnant. Additionally, when the guys interrupted Bathsheba's bath, she did not, perhaps, finish purifying herself and was still unclean. Perhaps the narrator is telling us that not only does David commit adultery, but he does so with a foreign woman. No one, then, should be surprised when Bathsheba is pregnant.

✦ The Gospel of Matthew highlights a theme of higher righteousness. It's not enough to restrain from physically pursuing the person for whom you lust. Jesus, like the pharisaic Jews of his time, holds us to a higher standard: don't even lust, don't even think about having sex with any person who belongs to another or if you yourself belong to another. Jesus is talking about the world as if God ruled—it is a utopian vision. In that perfect world, there is no adultery because there is no lust.

5 Caught in the act? Is she dressed? Is she alone? Yes, the law of Moses (Leviticus 20:10) does say that an adulteress should be killed, *and* it says that the adulterer should be killed as well. Where is the man? This is another occasion when Jesus is asked to make a legal decision and clarify his teachings according to the law of Moses. This question put to Jesus suggests that the idea of capital punishment for the offense of adultery was debated in Jesus's time, and perhaps earlier.

6 The religious leaders come to him with a question and Jesus changes the rules. He doesn't address the problem of adultery, he doesn't engage in a legal argument, and he doesn't judge her; rather, he changes the subject to the sins of all humanity. Jesus declares that only the sinless can inflict punishment. Jesus's first reaction indicates that he isn't going to respond as expected. He stoops down and writes in the dirt.

house. And the woman conceived; and she sent and told David, "I am with child."[4]

—2 SAMUEL 11:1–5

You have heard that it was said, "You shall not commit adultery." But I say to you that everyone who looks at a woman lustfully has already committed adultery with her in his heart.

—MATTHEW 5:27–28

They said to him, "Teacher, this woman has been caught in the act of adultery. Now in the law Moses commanded us to stone such. What do you say about her?"[5] This they said to test him, that they might have some charge to bring against him. Jesus bent down and wrote with his finger on the ground. And as they continued to ask him, he stood up and said to them, "Let him who is without sin among you be the first to throw a stone at her."[6] And once more he bent down and wrote with his finger on the ground. But when they heard it, they went away, one by one, beginning with the eldest, and Jesus was left alone with the woman

(continued on page 35)

7 The question I always want to ask of this passage is, how long does Jesus stoop down to write? Jesus has been teaching with throngs of people who have endured the hardships of travel to follow him. But the text tells us that Jesus stooped down for so long that eventually he was left *alone* with the woman. How long would it take for such an interested crowd to leave, one by one, until no one was left but Jesus? The elders must have thought that they were bringing Jesus the worst sinner they could find: an adulteress caught in the act.

8 For Jesus, to the elders' surprise, adultery is just another sin among sins; it is just another symptom of humanity in need of God. We might do well to remember that those sins that get us all twisted up and red in the face are, in the end, just sins like any other—though maybe our emotional reaction to them reveals an area in our own lives where we need more of God.

✦ What Jesus doesn't do here is of interest: he doesn't give lasting help to this woman. Is her marriage over? Since he forbids divorce, what will she do? Must she be celibate the rest of her life?

standing before him.[7] Jesus looked up and said to her,
"Woman, where are they? Has no one condemned you?"
She said, "No one, Lord." And Jesus said, "Neither do I
condemn you; go, and do not sin again."[8]

—JOHN 8:4–11

✦ The term "interracial" is anachronistic to the biblical texts. Our understanding of race is a modern construction and so, strictly speaking, the Bible doesn't address interracial anything. It does, however, address relationships between different cultures, religions, and ethnicities. Hence I use the term "interracial" loosely in order to indicate how these texts continue to have relevance for our own modern-day concerns.

1 The Hebrew Bible went through various editions as historical situations arose. The Deuteronomistic Historian (DH) was one of the Bible's consistent editors. The fingerprints of the editor are clear: no mixing with other cultures, and God punishes the entire people for the sins of the people. The word *toevah,* translated into English as "abomination," does not occur in this passage, but the idea behind it is here. The word means "mixing or confusion." The idea of mixing unlike things (seeds, clothing, species) was repulsive to the Israelites, and for good reason. Their cultural existence depended on their remaining separate (*qodesh*). In Leviticus 11:44–45, God tells them, "remain holy [*qodesh*] as I am holy." If the people remain holy (separate), they will be blessed. Being blessed means rainfall, food, protection from military destruction, and children. Moreover, the land of Canaan is populated and constantly overrun with invaders who are passing through. If Israel wishes to maintain religious and cultural purity, the Levitical purity codes make sense: no mixing. The bottom line is that the Israelites should not be tempted into cultures that worship different gods. Rather than risk idolatry, God commands them to kill the invaders: animals, men, women, and children—no mercy. This command (*herem* in Hebrew) directly contradicts God's other commandments not to kill or murder. Likewise, the author of Revelation, often referred to as John, uses the same motif: Those who mix with other cultures, who stray from the church, are dealt with violently.

2 As a recurring theme with the editors, as with the author of Revelation, sexual intercourse is practically synonymous with worshiping other deities. For the priests and prophets (including John the Revelator), who understand that a covenant with God is a marriage, there is little difference between intermarriage and idolatry.

Interracial Marriage

And when the Lord your God gives them over to you, and you defeat them; then you must utterly destroy them; you shall make no political agreement with them, and show no mercy to them.[1] You shall not make marriages with them, giving your daughters to their sons or taking their daughters for your sons. For they would turn away your sons from following me, to serve other gods; then the anger of the Lord would be kindled against you, and he would destroy you quickly.[2]

—DEUTERONOMY 7:2–3

Therefore let us make a covenant with our God to put away all these wives and their children, according to the counsel of my lord and of those who tremble [in fear] at the commandment of our God; and let it be done according to the law.

—EZRA 10:3

✦ The Prophets determined that the exile—that is, when the people of Judah were forced out of their promised land—was a direct result of idolatry, their "whoring" with foreign gods. After the exile a series of priests and kings set about to rebuild the Temple so as to reestablish proper worship and reinstate the lost separateness/holiness. Ezra's proclamation to annul all marriages to foreign women is his first divisive wedge. Symbolically, the foreign woman is transformed into a promiscuous and dangerous seductress. By ending intermarriage Ezra metaphorically and literally rebuilds a wall of separation between the Israelites and those who worship other gods.

✦ One of the Bible's views of foreigners—that they are wicked and should be destroyed, and if someone mixes with them, that person will be cut off from God's blessings or even killed—is certainly one of the strongest messages that comes out in the Hebrew Bible. However, it is not the only attitude about foreigners. The book of Ruth is one of several books in the Hebrew Bible that speak favorably of foreigners and marriage with them. Ruth is a Moabite, a foreign woman, who marries an Israelite man, Mahlon. Ruth's husband dies, so she travels with her mother-in-law to Bethlehem and finds a husband among the people there (again, an Israelite). There is no problem whatsoever here of intermarriage. In fact, much of the Bible shows no concern at all with mixed marriages. Joseph, Moses, Esther—all major characters—have foreign partners.

We learn at the end of the book of Ruth that through the line of Ruth and Boaz (her second Israelite husband) comes the greatest king of Israel, David. It is a strong defense of the goodness of foreigners, with no warning about intermarriage.

✦ This passage offers a good model for people who are in an interracial, intercultural, or intergenerational (Boaz was much older than Ruth) marriage. It is a story of a loving family. The story never criticizes Ruth as a foreigner, and it never comments on her class or her age. She is the model mother and her favor with God is shown through her progeny.

These took Moabite wives; the name of the one was Orpah and the name of the other Ruth. They lived there about ten years.

—RUTH 1:4

Now these are the descendants of Perez: Perez was the father of Hezron, Hezron of Ram, Ram of Ammin'adab, Ammin'adab of Nahshon, Nahshon of Salmon, Salmon of Bo'az, Bo'az of Obed, Obed of Jesse, and Jesse of David.

—RUTH 4:18–22

3 The word I've translated here as "mismatched" doesn't have a modern English equivalent. It roughly refers to two beasts that are yoked together to pull a plow, but are mismatched in strength. The unequal force of their pulling means they will move in a circle instead of a straight line. The author of this passage goes on to make a case that a stronger one should never be paired with a lesser, weaker one.

4 From the language that Paul uses, we see that his thinking is right in line with the Deuteronomist above (7:2–3). The fear for Paul is the same as the fear for the priests of Israel: mixing with persons of other faiths may lead to idolatry or, worse, syncretism—a watering down of the true faith.

✦ While the Bible's editors believed that the Israelites' and the early Christians' survival may have depended on staying separate, I doubt this was ever possible. Some modern religious groups have depended on this rhetoric to argue that racial separation is ordained by God. The Southern Baptist Convention officially withdrew their ban on interracial marriage in the 1960s. However, many quasi-religious groups in the Christian Identity movement continue to spread hate by using the Bible to forbid interracial relationships. Yet the difference for us today is that human survival depends on our mixing with other cultures, which is manifested in the freedom to marry the person of one's choosing. It is, as the Genesis creation and the early church architects claimed about marriage in general, the foundation of a stable world. Though these verses have been used to prohibit interracial marriages, Paul's primary concern is interreligious marriage. He argues to dissuade (not forbid) Christians marrying non-Christians.

✦ The Bible has no single attitude toward foreigners. Regardless of whether the Bible affirms positive relationships with foreigners (as we see in the stories of Jonah, Ruth, Esther, and others) or forbids interaction, particular attitudes regarding foreigners are certainly no longer applicable to us today. These ideas come from a time when the foreigner represented catastrophe—at least, that's the way the priests and John the Revelator saw it. We've learned that survival actually depends on having good and loving relationships with other nations, other races, and other ethnicities.

Do not be mismatched with unbelievers. For what partnership have righteousness and iniquity? Or what fellowship has light with darkness? What accord has Christ with Satan? Or what has a believer in common with an unbeliever? What agreement has the temple of God with idols? For we are the temple of the living God; as God said, "I will live in them and move among them, and I will be their God, and they shall be my people.[3] Therefore come out from them, and be separate from them, says the Lord, and touch nothing unclean;[4] then I will welcome you and I will be a father to you, and you shall be my sons and daughters, says the Lord Almighty."

—2 CORINTHIANS 6:14–18

1 David is old and the lover his servants seek for him is awfully young. There is no restriction on how many years apart a man and woman must be to have sex. Here, it is the remedy sought for a lifeless king.

✦ Passages like this show us that sexual "heat" is recognized, even in the Bible, as having some sort of healing benefits.

2 Boaz sees Ruth as blessed because she didn't go after young men but held out for a rich old man.

✦ There are several examples of older men taking much younger women as brides (e.g., Isaac and Rebekah, Genesis 25:20–26; Jacob and Rachel, Genesis 29:18). Women were usually betrothed before they started menstruating and were married when they hit puberty (twelve or thirteen). However, I do not know of any passage in the Bible in which an older woman has a younger husband. In Genesis 38, Judah refuses to let Tamar marry his youngest son.

✦ Today there is a double standard for intergenerational marriage. We are more accustomed to seeing older men marry younger women than the other way around. Our culture seems more supportive of such arrangements. Many films depict much older men having relationships with young women (though we can never forget the sultry Mrs. Robinson). But these are cultural attitudes that probably developed from the fact that men can produce fertile sperm long after women can conceive. And, perhaps, that the older male still occupies the place of elite power. These biblical passages remind us that not much has changed regarding cultural attitudes of power in sexual relationships, but it does not restrict with whom we can choose to have a lasting and loving sexual relationship.

☐ Intergenerational Relationships

Now King David was old and sickly and they covered him with lots of blankets but he still couldn't get warm. Then, his servants said, "Let's find a young virgin for you.[1] Make her stand in front of you and she will lust for you. She will lie with you and you will get warm."

—1 KINGS 1:1–4

He said, "May you be blessed by the Lord, my daughter; this last example of your loyalty is better than the first; you have not gone after young men, whether poor or rich."[2]

—RUTH 3:10

1 Having and not having children was seen as reward or punishment from God. In the Hebrew Bible, a child, especially a son, is a sign of God's blessing. In the New Testament, having children is a woman's salvation (1 Timothy 2:15).

2 Abraham owns both Sarah and Sarah's servant, Hagar. He has sexual privileges with both women. However, since Sarah is the primary wife, she also has some control over Hagar's sexuality. The custom is that if Hagar actually births the child on Sarah's lap, the baby belongs to Sarah.

3 Abraham had other wives besides Sarah and Hagar. The Bible doesn't mention them much; they're not as important to the grand narrative of Abraham and the Israelites. But the Bible doesn't defend or apologize for his having multiple wives. It is the custom of the time. As a wealthy and powerful man, it is not only Abraham's right to have several wives but an emblem of his power. A man would be measured by his possessions: slaves, mules, women. Women are still a measure of a man's success; for today's bachelor, having more than one sexual partner may be seen as an honor rather than a shame (it's usually the opposite for women). Today men are required to marry women sequentially rather than all at once. Some might consider a series of failed marriages as defeats, but others see them as "notches in the belt."

4 The sons of the primary wives are the most important—they inherit everything. The rest receive gifts and are sent away.

5 Jacob, like his grandfather Abraham, had several wives. He has two primary wives and two lesser wives. Nevertheless, the Bible again offers no defense for this. In fact, it is a sign of God's blessing that Jacob has so many wives who can produce so many sons for him.

Multiple Wives and Husbands

Sarah said to Abraham, "Look, the Lord has prevented me from having a child.[1] I beg you, go in to my woman; she could have a child on my lap," and Abraham took her advice.[2]

—GENESIS 16:2

Abraham gave all he had to Isaac. But to the sons of his concubines Abraham gave gifts,[3] while he was still living, and he sent them away from his son Isaac,[4] eastwards to the east country.

—GENESIS 25:5–6

Give me [Jacob] my wives and my children for whom I have served you,[5] and let me go; for you know very well the service I have given you.

—GENESIS 30:26

✦ The verse from Genesis 30 and similar verses have been used for justification of polygamy. These are simply not applicable. They belong to a different cultural mind-set in which women are property and considered evidence of wealth and God's blessings on men. The Qur'an has a similar, though confusing, teaching about multiple wives. Muhammad teaches that a man could marry several wives if he could treat them all equally. Some argue that this alone amounts to a prohibition of polygamy, while others see it as permitted.

6 The author of Judges accepts polygamy as a normal way of life for Gideon.

✦ The greater the king, the more wives he should have. The possessions showed his wealth, but more importantly, each wife was a connection to a foreign power. A king's political alliances were sealed through a marriage. She became a token of treaties, real estate arrangements, and other negotiations. Any king worth his salt would have perhaps hundreds of wives. The wives functioned much like Elvis's Cadillacs: they were the symbols and gifts of an extremely powerful man.

7 Absalom is David's son. His friend Ahithophel is advising him to have sex with his father's concubines. Absalom, whose name means "my father is peace," understands completely that the women are his father's property and to have sex with them is, ultimately, an attack on his father, an attack on peace.

8 As a symbol of the power of a man, to "take" one of David's concubines would directly challenge his honor. Absalom is picking a fight.

Now Gideon had seventy sons, his own offspring, for he had many wives.[6]

—JUDGES 8:30

In Jerusalem, after he came from Hebron, David took more concubines and wives; and more sons and daughters were born to David.

—2 SAMUEL 5:13

Ahithophel said to Ab'salom, "Go in to your father's concubines,[7] the ones he has left to look after the house; and all Israel will hear that you have made yourself odious to your father, and the hands of all who are with you will be strengthened."[8]

—2 SAMUEL 16:21

9 While a man's honor was reflected in how many wives and concubines he had, a concubine's honor was wrapped up in giving sexual pleasure to her master. For David not to have sex with these concubines was extremely shameful for them. He made sure they had food, water, and anything else they needed to survive, but they could not leave the house (which meant no opportunity for sex with anyone else). He ultimately deprived them of honor.

10 This would have been the ultimate punishment for a concubine. David's concubines had no chance for honor and they lived as widows: mourning their youth, never giving sexual pleasure to David. The author never imagines that they could just have sex with one another.

11 Solomon was clearly the model of all powerful men. The author of 1 Kings wants us to know that Solomon was the Donald Trump of his time: mighty building projects, lots of desirable wives (though Solomon had his all at once), and much gold. The concubines demonstrated his sheer wealth through possessions, and the princess brides showed his political power. The Bible's authors do not approve of Solomon's many foreign wives.

12 God's jealousy of Solomon is the real problem. The Hebrew Bible's writers do not care how many wives a man takes; the real issue is that they are foreign women. If a king takes foreign women as brides, they will seduce him away from his first wife, God.

✦ When you consult the Bible on culturally and temporally specific practices like polygamy, it just doesn't work. The Bible should not be the only marriage manual for us today. Our social customs about meeting, marrying, and having sex (not always in this order), along with what is in our hearts, should be our fundamental guide today—the Bible should be a supplementary guide. The Bible is an excellent historical source for the social customs of an ancient people who are far, far away from the United States. But it isn't helpful for modern daily living, with its allusions to having babies with your wives. This simply isn't the life we lead today.

David came to his house at Jerusalem; and the king took the ten concubines whom he had left to look after the house, and put them in a house under guard, and provided for them, but did not go in to them.[9] So they were shut up until the day of their death, living as if they were widows.[10]

—2 SAMUEL 20:3

Among [Solomon's] wives were seven hundred princesses and three hundred concubines;[11] and his wives turned away his heart [from God].[12]

—1 KINGS 11:3

13 You might assume that the Samaritan woman is some sort of immoral woman, or at least a serial divorcée. The text, however, doesn't support a negative reading of the woman. Perhaps her previous husbands have died from disease or war. Maybe the man she is now with is her brother or father. Later conversation with Jesus shows that her primary concerns (after water) are theological.

14 The woman's community also finds her to be a trustworthy source. Early Christian fathers and modern interpretations have portrayed this woman as a sexually immoral person to whom Jesus offers forgiveness. There are many circumstances that can contribute to a woman's necessity to remarry, though five times seems odd. Nevertheless, there is no comment by Jesus or by the Samaritan woman's peers on her multiple marriages; the sexual slanders come primarily by later Christian readers.

Jesus said to her, "Go, call your husband, and come back." The woman answered him, "I have no husband." Jesus said to her, "you have spoken well saying, 'I have no husband'; for you have had five husbands [or men], and the one you have now is not your husband.[13] What you have said is true." ... Many Samaritans from that city believed in him because of the woman's testimony, "He told me everything I have ever done."[14]

—JOHN 4:16–18; 39

1 David (see Adultery) looks across the way at a beautiful woman bathing. If the story had stopped there, in verse 2, when David was only looking, there would be no harm, no foul. This verse doesn't say that he admires her beauty, desires her, or that he intends to do anything; we only know that he sees her and that she is beautiful.

2 David crosses the line in verse 4: he sees her, he desires her, and he takes her. Today, many people would assume that there's no harm in looking. In fact, at times it almost seems rude not to look and comment on someone's appearance. In other cultures, however, a look can be disrespectful or even an aggressive act.

✦ Since private bathing in any ancient city was probably next to impossible, women must have had to depend on and expect the courtesy of other people averting their eyes at one time or another. David's first misstep is his impudent gaze, not his desire. There is also no mention of love in this passage.

✦ David is a powerful man and is accustomed to getting what he wants. On the other hand, who is to say that Bathsheba didn't want to have sex with David? He gets Bathsheba, has sex with her, and sends her home. If she hadn't become pregnant, the story would not catch the attention of anyone.

Lust, Passion, and Desire

It happened, late one afternoon, when David arose from sleeping and was walking upon the roof of the king's house, that he saw from the roof a woman bathing; and the woman was very beautiful.[1] So David sent messengers, and took her [fetched, snatched];[2] and she came to him, and he lay with her. (Now she was purifying herself from her uncleanness.) Then she returned to her house.

—2 SAMUEL 11:2, 4

3 Amnon, like his father David, gazed and desired a forbidden woman (see Leviticus 18:11). Both of these passages make the point in English that the woman was beautiful. Perhaps this is to suggest that because of the woman's beauty, the men could not help themselves. However, both words that have been translated as "beautiful" can also mean "pleasant." While the text is more clear in the case of Bathsheba (she was pleasant to look at), Amnon could have been in love with Tamar because she was a pleasant person—this doesn't necessarily mean physical beauty. Translators opt for "beauty" here because the beauty of the women turns the men into victims of seduction, or persons who cannot control themselves, rather than sexual aggressors.

✦ It would be a good thing for us to recognize that lust can often be more similar to hate than it is to love. If we desire a person, our desire sometimes turns that person into an object. Already we've committed a kind of murder by stripping away the humanity from him or her.

✦ In Song of Songs, lust, passion, and sexual desire are exceedingly good things. They bring pleasure, they bring happiness in knowing that you belong to someone and that someone belongs to you, and they bring song. Lao Tzu expressed a similar notion as the lover in Song of Songs when he wrote, "To love someone deeply gives you strength; to be loved deeply by someone gives you courage."

Now Ab'salom, David's son, had a beautiful sister, whose name was Tamar; and after a time Amnon, David's son, loved her.[3] And Amnon was so distressed that he made himself ill because of his sister Tamar; for she was a virgin, and it seemed impossible to Amnon to do anything to her.

—2 SAMUEL 13:1–2

4 As a Pharisee and as a Roman citizen, Paul knows that God has commanded us to be holy. The Hebrew word for holy, *qodesh,* literally means "separate or apart," which becomes quite a literal matter in terms of food, worship, and sex. For example, different types of seeds are not sown together; and the followers of God do not mix with the followers of other gods. But Paul knows that indeed, Jews and Gentiles have worshiped together in the past. There are historical references to "godfearers"—Gentiles who were welcomed into synagogues in worship of God. Paul plays the holiness card often in his letters to new Christians since they were already familiar with categories of holiness. He is faced with the enormous task of unifying a diverse group of people. Paul appeals to the priestly categories of food and sex. In this verse he is specifically appealing to sexual control. In order to live peacefully within a diverse community, you must control your sexual passions.

5 To be "holy," a person must not participate in *porneia*—sexual excess. The meaning of *porneia* shifts depending on who is doing the interpreting. *Porneia* is all sex that is "out of place"; normal, however, is in the eye of the beholder. The problem is, who gets to determine what constitutes excess?

I am my beloved's, and his desire is for me.

—SONG OF SONGS 7:10

For this is the will of God, your own holiness:[4] that you refrain from sexual excesses;[5] that each one of you knows

(continued on page 59)

6 For more guidance on shunning *porneia,* Paul tells us that keeping your *skevos,* literally "spoon" or "bowl," in holiness is the way to avoid sexual wrongdoing. Paul is using it metaphorically, of course, but it is not surprising that he is using a culinary term to talk about sex, since these are the two primary categories of purity. Various translators of this verse have called it "implement," "tool," "member," "vessel," "body," and "wife." Paul urges *self*-control here.

7 Paul does not condemn sex, lust, or passion; he merely requires that each person control his or her own passions.

✦ Paul and Jesus do not agree on the matter of lust. For Paul, passions are acceptable if they are controlled. For Jesus, lust is unacceptable. Jesus's teachings are for the ideal world, the world if God ruled it. For Paul, lust is inevitable; the best we can do is channel it appropriately by getting married.

how to keep his or her own vessel[6] in holiness and honor, not in the passion of lust like heathens who do not know God.[7]

—1 Thessalonians 4:3–7

1 Earlier, in Genesis 18:2, three "men" visit with Abraham in the cool of the evening beneath the grove at Mamre. We always assume that these men are angels, since they seem to represent the Lord, but the Hebrew is "men." At the end of chapter 18, we are told that these men then turn toward Sodom, which God is about to destroy because of some unknown wickedness (Genesis 13:13). We are not given any details regarding the sins of Sodom. Though the sins of Sodom have historically been assumed to involve homosexuality, the Prophets did not have this understanding. Isaiah, for example, does not tell us what he thinks the sin of Sodom is. His complaint is that they do not hide it; that they are proud in their sin (Isaiah 3:9). Jeremiah writes that the sins of Sodom are adultery, lying, and a refusal to stop (Jeremiah 23:14). Ezekiel is clear and sure about the sins of Sodom: Sodom had pride, a surplus of food, and an easy, luxurious life, but did not aid the poor and needy (Ezekiel 16:49). If God is destroying Sodom for the sin of homosexuality, as we have assumed for centuries, the prophets, the voices of God, make no mention of it. As chapter 19 of Genesis begins, verse 1 tells us that only two "messengers" are heading to Sodom. If these are the same agents of God from Genesis 18, where's the third one?

2 We see that Lot, like his uncle Abraham, shows utmost hospitality to the messengers. He offers a foot washing, surely a soothing necessity for travelers in those days. He prepares a feast for them and gives them a place to sleep.

3 *All* of the people of Sodom surround Lot's house. Traditionally in interpretations of this story, the "crowd" around Lot's house is assumed to be entirely male. But the Hebrew word here, *enosh,* means the generic, nongender-specific person, or humankind. In fact, the Hebrew makes it clear that "all of the people" of Sodom surrounded the house (in contrast to *zakar,* which would indicate the male person).

☐ Sexual Orientation

The two messengers[1] came to Sodom in the evening; and Lot was sitting in the gate of Sodom. When Lot saw them, he rose to meet them, and bowed himself with his face to the earth, and said, "My lords, turn aside, I beg you, to your servant's house and spend the night, and wash your feet; then you may rise up early and go on your way." They said, "No; we will spend the night in the street." But he insisted; so they turned aside to him and entered his house; and he made them a feast, and baked unleavened bread, and they ate.[2] But before they lay down, the people of the city, the people of Sodom, both young and old, all the people to the last person, surrounded the house;[3] and they called to Lot,

(continued on page 63)

4 So, all of the people, male and female, surround Lot's house. They demand that Lot send out the messengers to them so that they may "know" them. "To know" (*yada*) is a common euphemism for sex in the Bible, so that this is what the crowd meant is the general assumption by most readers, though it should not be the only one. You could read this literally: the people of Sodom may have an inkling that God intends to destroy them and they want some answers. Perhaps they intend sexual violence; maybe they want information. Faced with immanent destruction, it would certainly be an expected and reasonable reaction for the people of Sodom to threaten the strangers with violence. We can never know why the people of Sodom call out their certain destroyers, but if you consider their destiny, it does make sense. Maybe it is a show of power, such as, for example, a brutal prison rape.

5 Lot begs the crowd not to harm his guests, and in a surprising and shocking move, he offers them his own virgin daughters instead. Even though this passage has long been used to condemn homosexuality, it has not been used to condemn sexual violence against women. This passage shows that ancient attitudes about women and sexuality are peculiar to us today. The people of Sodom reject the virgin women. Their rejection shows that sex per se isn't on their mind, but rather, they are more interested in interrogating, punishing, or overpowering the messengers of God's destruction. Later events demonstrate that the biblical writers themselves disapproved of Lot's offering.

✦ The rejection of Lot's daughters causes the cultural suspicion of this story. Readers wonder why a sexually "normal" male would reject sexual intercourse with a virgin. But if you think about it, the story goes like this: two men come to destroy a city; all the people of the city surround their house; Lot offers his daughters for sex, but that isn't what the people want. As they make a threatening move toward the house, the messengers blind them and destroy the city. Where is the homosexuality in this story? The bottom line is this: we have all received standard interpretations of certain Bible passages, but are these always the correct and only ones? When we look closer, we often see that things aren't necessarily as we were taught.

"Where are the men who came to you tonight? Bring them
out to us, that we may know them."**4** Lot went out of the
door to the men, shut the door after him, and said, "I beg
you, my kin, do not act so wickedly. Behold, I have two
daughters who have not known man; let me bring them out
to you, and do to them as you please; only do nothing to
these men, for they have come under the shelter of my
roof."**5** But they said, "Stand back!" And they said, "This
fellow came as a guest, and he would play the judge! Now
we will deal worse with you than with them." Then they
pressed hard against the man Lot, and drew near to break
the door. But the men put out their hands and brought Lot
into the house to them, and shut the door. And they struck
with blindness the ones who were at the door of the house,
both small and great, so that they wearied themselves
groping for the door.

—GENESIS 19:1–11

6 Even though the translation is vague, its meaning is clear: men who have sex with men shall be killed. This verse requires that we consider the word *abomination,* and why death is an "appropriate" response here.

7 There is much more to this verse than meets the eye. The word *toevah,* usually translated here as abomination, means "mixing" or "confusion." The idea of mixing unlike things (e.g., seeds, clothing, species) was repulsive and dangerous to the Israelites. Their cultural and physical existence, as they saw it, depended on remaining separate. Staying separate meant not only keeping apart from other peoples, but also keeping all things in their proper categories. The "confusion" of homoerotic sex is that two unlike things mix together. I know you're thinking, "How are two men unlike things?" In male-to-male sex, one man must be the active partner and one man is penetrated. In the minds of the Israelite priests, passivity is not natural for men; for a man to be the passive sexual partner, he must act like a woman. The two categories that become confused are *man* and *woman.* According to Leviticus, a man who acts like a woman is *toevah*.

8 The death sentence seems harsh to us for sexual intercourse, yet the Israelites would have understood that this sexual act was equal to the death sentence for the whole community. In situations when the survival of the whole community is threatened, the offending "thing" is extracted and destroyed. If these ideas sound strange and foreign, it's because they are. Making sure that things stay in their proper categories to the point of executing the person who confuses categories is not something we do today.

✦ These codes are not for us today. Our whole survival does not depend on staying separate and not confusing categories. Even if they were, it would be impossible today (as it probably was in ancient Israel). These laws were more than likely never implemented. They were probably adopted from other cultures and used more as deterrents than anything else.

If a man lies with a male as with a woman,[6] both of them have committed confusion;[7] they shall be put to death,[8] their blood is upon them.

—LEVITICUS 20:1

✦ Once we understand the mind-set of the Israelites on the dangers of mixing categories (see Leviticus 20:13), a prohibition of cross-dressing or transvestitism, as found in Deuteronomy 22:5, makes sense to us (as much as we can make sense of ancient purity codes). Ensuring that everything stays in its proper place usually means, above all, gendered categories.

✦ Finally the question remains: what does this have to do with you and your choices about sex? And to that I would say: nothing and something. The cultic laws in the Bible were rules for a particular people. As a gardener, I never consult these laws as I sow my seeds; and when I'm dressing to go out, I never peek at Leviticus to determine what to wear. Nor do I look at Leviticus for information on sex. Still, these are rules that worked to create and maintain community. If we try to live in a community, particularly one whose survival depends on cooperation and interdependency (the community of humanity, for example), it is imperative that we abide by agreed-upon rules concerning food, clothing, shelter, and, of course, sex. If I don't understand a rule, or even if I don't agree with it, there may be a meaning to it that reaches beyond me as an individual; it may be a rule that is designed for the good of the whole group, not the individual. The rules of Leviticus about sex, food, and various other things, however, are not one-size-fits-all for any culture. They are particular to a specific people in a particular place and time.

9 It is difficult not to see homoeroticism just below the surface in this passage. If this description of love had been about a woman and a man, no one would think twice about romantic intent.

10 In a covenant (a contract) there was often an exchange of items, for security or collateral, though Jonathan's gifs to David here seem excessively abundant. He gives David his most prized and necessary possessions. His robe would be the literal coat of arms of his royalty, the presumed future king. His armor, sword, and bow would have been his favorites, the only things that stand between him and death.

(continued on page 68)

When David had finished speaking to Saul, the soul of Jonathan was bound to the soul of David, and Jonathan loved him as his own soul.[9] Saul took him that day and would not let him return to his father's house. Then Jonathan made a covenant with David, because he loved him as his own soul. Jonathan stripped himself of the robe that he was wearing, and gave it to David, and his armor, and even his sword and his bow and his belt.[10]

—1 SAMUEL 18:1–4

Through this covenant and these gestures, Jonathan is declaring a lasting and loyal devotion to David, even at the expense of his own life.

11 Saul is calling Jonathan the equivalent to our slanderous "son of a bitch."

12 Saul later threatens to take away all of Jonathan's inheritance, including the kingdom of Israel, because he loves David. Jonathan ends up choosing David over his family.

13 Saul is making it clear that Jonathan's love and devotion to David is shameful, not only to himself but also to his mother. The phrase "to your mother's nakedness" is in reference to Jonathan's conception. In other words, Saul is saying to Jonathan that it would be better if he were never conceived.

✦ The tirade of Saul against his son Jonathan over his love for David is a far too familiar one for many gays and lesbians. For many who have come out to their parents, they withstand a barrage of curses, name-calling, slanders, shaming, and guilt-tripping. In spite of Saul's poisonous rant, Jonathan continues to love David.

14 Two men holding each other, kissing, and weeping is not an image we expect to find in the Bible. This is David's final good-bye to his beloved soul mate.

Then Saul's anger was kindled against Jonathan. He said to him, "You son of a perverse, rebellious woman![11] Don't I know that you have chosen the son of Jesse[12] to your own shame, and to the shame of your mother's nakedness?[13]

—1 SAMUEL 20:30

As soon as the boy had gone, David rose from beside the stone heap and prostrated himself with his face to the ground. He bowed three times, and they kissed each other, and wept with each other; David wept the more.[14]

—1 SAMUEL 20:41

15 Upon hearing of Jonathan's death, David mournfully declares that he loved Jonathan more than any woman. David later becomes infamous for his many wives and an adulterous and murderous relationship with a married woman. A common misconception about sexuality is that a person has desire for only one gender. The modern idea of a homosexual is a person who chooses one sex at the exclusion of the other. One of the lessons we can take from the story of Jonathan and David is that men who marry and who father children may also harbor sexual desires for other men.

✦ Homoeroticism in the ancient world, particularly after Hellenism, was not something that only "certain" men did exclusively. An aristocratic man would most likely have had a wife, a mistress, and a younger male lover.

16 God allows the chief eunuch to have tender love and, therefore, compassion for Daniel. That way, Daniel can serve God by keeping the laws. If the eunuch did not have feelings for Daniel, he would have forced him to eat the forbidden food, removed him from the palace, or even had him killed. The Lord indeed works in mysterious ways. This passage suggests that a man's desire for another man is something that God created; it is depicted here as something useful for continuing the worship of God.

I am distraught for you, my brother Jonathan; I loved you so much; your love to me was wonderful, passing the love of women.[15]

—2 SAMUEL 1:26

Now God allowed Daniel to receive favor and tender love from the chief eunuch.[16]

—DANIEL 1:9

17 Paul has the enormous responsibility of unifying diverse peoples within Christian communities. This passage in Romans—the only passage in the Bible that mentions female homoeroticism—is not as clear as it could be because it is only a part of a larger argument that Paul is putting forward. But make no mistake, Paul does not like homoeroticism, and he is concerned in this passage particularly with sex among women. We see a decidedly Hellenistic influence in his ideas about sexuality and gender; Paul's attitudes about homoeroticism are firmly in sync with, according to Bernadette Brooten, his Greek contemporaries.

✦ Today we know that gender markers (the clothes we wear, how we wear our hair, our jewelry, and even how we walk) are things that are specific to our culture, not something we are born with or that is "natural" for us. In Europe men commonly wear Capri pants—pants that reach only to about midshin—yet most of my Missouri-born male friends have remarked that they cannot even *imagine* wearing such "girl" pants; what seems unnatural to them is an everyday occurrence in Italy. For Paul, as a Hellenistic Jew and as a product of his culture, gender markers are "natural." He has commonly held assumptions about human sexuality: men are active penetrators, women are passive receptors. If women have sex with women, Paul assumes that one must take on an active, that is, masculine, "penetrating" role. In Paul's eyes, this is "unnatural."

✦ Paul's thinking seems to be that God's response to the unwillingness of gentiles to do what is natural and worship Him, is to let them do whatever unnatural thing they choose. In other words, by not keeping the first law—to have one and only one God, Paul's God—they are free from all of God's laws. Most people don't read the rest of the passage. Paul goes on in Romans 2 to criticize the Jewish Christians for passing judgment on those gentiles. Paul's final point in Romans 3 is this: yes, gentiles have "unnatural" sex, and yes, you have sinned by judging them; therefore *all* have sinned and fallen short of the glory of God.

For the anger of God is revealed from heaven against all profanity and wickedness of men who by their wickedness suppress the truth. For what can be known about God is plain to them, because God has shown it to them. Ever since the creation of the world his invisible nature, namely, his eternal power and divinity, has been clearly perceived in the things that have been made. So they are without excuse; for although they knew God they did not honor him as God or give thanks to him, but they became futile in their thinking and their senseless minds were darkened. Claiming to be wise, they became fools, and exchanged the glory of the immortal God for images resembling humans or birds or animals or reptiles. Therefore God gave them up in the lusts of their hearts to impurity, to the dishonoring of their bodies among themselves, because they exchanged the truth about God for a lie and worshiped and served the creature rather than the Creator, who is blessed for ever! Amen. For this reason God gave them up to dishonorable passions. Their women exchanged natural relations for unnatural,[17] and the men likewise gave up natural relations with women and were consumed with passion for one another, men committing shameless acts with men and receiving in their own persons the due penalty for their error.

—ROMANS 1:18–27

✦ Most of us today do not think about gender and sex like Paul does. The Romans 1 passage reminds us that Paul believed that rejecting God's natural order (as he understood it in this cultural and historical context) and rejecting God were one and the same. And since this passage occurs at the beginning of Romans and is always taken out of context from the rest of his argument, it is hard to see that he is laying an excellent foundation for a defense of Christian rejection of Mosaic law. The bigger point is this: Paul understands sexual relationships in precisely the same ways that others in his culture understand them. His writings on homoeroticism are much in line with other writings of educated, elite males of his time. But since we don't accept all of Paul's cultural assumptions (such as fashion, hairstyles, occupations), why should we accept the ones on sex?[3]

18 I specifically translated the word that is usually translated as "effeminate men," "homosexuals," or "sexual perverts" (*malakoi*) as its literal meaning: soft men. We cannot know exactly what Paul means by using a word such as "soft men," which may be a local colloquialism. When *malakos* (sing.) is used in other Greco-Roman literature, it does allude to men who have too many feminine traits. It has been used, for example, to describe men who may pay to much attention to their own bodies in order to seduce women. Even to say that he could mean impotent men is at least true to Paul's Hellenistic understanding of sex and masculinity and would fit with Paul's view of sexual inadequacy as unnatural.

✦ We can see in Romans that Paul saw homoeroticism as unclean; he saw it as something the pagans did because they didn't know the real God and, therefore, the "natural" way to act. However, I believe Paul did not see homoeroticism as a distinct sin, like murder or adultery, but rather as an offense against the way things should be, the natural order of the world. We continue to make laws limiting the civil rights of homosexuals (just as, in the recent past, we made laws limiting the rights of African Americans and of women) based on murky and sometimes false translations. At the very least, these alternative interpretations I am offering show us that we must be careful with how we use the Bible. The translation or interpretation we know may not be the only one and it may not be the right one.

Don't you know that the unrighteous will not inherit the kingdom of God? Do not be deceived; neither the immoral, nor idolaters, nor adulterers, nor soft men,[18] nor thieves, nor the greedy, nor drunkards, nor partiers, nor robbers will inherit the kingdom of God.

—1 CORINTHIANS 6:9–10

1 The Hebrew word for "eunuch" and for "army officer" is the same: *saris.* Sometimes it is translated one way and sometimes, the other. There doesn't seem to be any rhyme or reason about how the word is translated except as it applies to gender; if the *saris* is attending to women, it is usually translated as eunuch. If the *saris* is serving a superior male (king, captain), it is translated as officer. Since the title *saris* shows up forty-two times in the Hebrew Bible and is always given to a man whose job is to control others, I am convinced that the word suggests that any important man in the service of Pharaoh or any other leader would probably have been a eunuch. This would ensure a higher level of trust and require a single-minded devotion on the part of the servant. There were probably at least four, rather than two, genders in parts of the ancient world: men and women who reproduce, and men and women who do not, by choice, reproduce.

✦ The connection of our sex (our genitals) to our gender (behaving like men or like women) is a complex one. Today we may think it is as simple as this: "I have a vagina, I am a woman, so I should behave a certain way and I have specific roles in society," or, "I have a penis, I am a man, so I should behave a certain way and I have specific roles in society." In the ancient world, simply having a penis or a vagina did not necessarily make you a man or a woman. You had to have a *functioning* penis or vagina to be a man or a woman.

2 Ashpenaz is the chief officer over all of the men who serve the king. He and all the men he administers are more than likely eunuchs. (See Genesis 37:36.)

3 The king requests that the best and the brightest Israelite boys be brought to join his court in the palace. Daniel, then, was probably a eunuch himself, or at least made one in the Babylonian court; he was a handsome, smart, and physically fit young man destined to serve at the pleasure of the king.

Celibacy and Eunuchs

And the Midianites sold [Joseph] into Egypt unto Potiphar a eunuch[1] of Pharaoh and a captain of the guard.

—GENESIS 37:36

Then the king commanded Ashpenaz, head eunuch,[2] to bring some of the Israelites of the royal family and of the nobility, young men without physical defect and handsome, versed in every branch of wisdom, endowed with knowledge and insight, and competent to serve in the king's palace; they were to be taught the literature and language of the Chaldeans. The king assigned them a daily portion of the royal rations of food and wine. They were to be educated for three years, so that at the end of that time they could be stationed in the king's court.[3] Among them

(continued on page 79)

4 Daniel, though a physically and intellectually superior young man who had been handpicked by the king, is also devoutly religious. Even though the king provides Daniel with ample food and good wine daily, Daniel asks permission to eat his own food, prepared his own way. Daniel keeps kosher even among affluence and abundance.

5 The Hebrew here, *rakham,* means a deep, almost motherly love. It is associated with the womb as well as compassion. It is usually used in the Bible to talk about a love that is nurturing: God's love for humanity and a mother's love for her children.

6 Matthew tells us that some choose to be a eunuch for religious reasons. Perhaps it is the single-minded focus formerly demanded by monarchs and now demanded by God. The phrase "to become a eunuch for the kingdom of heaven" was understood by some early Christian Fathers to mean that some may choose to become celibate for the sake of becoming closer to God. The Greek word *eunouxos,* like its Hebrew counterpart, not only means a castrated male but also someone who has control over the comings and goings of the bedchambers. Eunuch means both chamberlain and castrated male simultaneously. It is provocative to think that the kingdom of God has a bedchamber and that God has the need for someone to control the goings-on in there. And since the eunuch typically works for the sovereign ruler and controls the sexuality of his many wives, in this case God is the king and someone is needed to safeguard the sexuality of God's lovers, the Christians, who have traditionally been the metaphorical wives of God.

✦ What is most obvious here is the Gospel's omission of any comment about Jesus's own sex life. A typical Jewish male would be expected to marry and have children: it is a sign of God's blessing. Jesus may have been celibate, for any number of reasons, but this was not a concern of the gospel writers. Jesus's sexuality came into sharper focus centuries later when original sin became a central concern, a theological invention that is infused with the cultural assumption that sex is a sin. The logic is: if sex is a sin and Jesus is perfect—well, no sex for Jesus. In fact, according to Matthew, Jesus could not have even *thought* about sex without sinning.

were Daniel, Hananiah, Mishael, and Azariah, from the tribe of Judah. The chief eunuch gave them other names: Daniel he called Belteshazzar, Hananiah he called Shadrach, Mishael he called Meshach, and Azariah he called Abednego. But Daniel resolved that he would not defile himself with the royal rations of food and wine; so he asked the chief eunuch to allow him not to defile himself.[4] Now God allowed Daniel to receive favor and tender love[5] from the chief eunuch.

—DANIEL 1:3–9

For there are eunuchs who have been so from birth, and there are eunuchs who have been made eunuchs by others, and there are eunuchs who have made themselves eunuchs for the sake of the kingdom of heaven. Let anyone hear this who can.[6]

—MATTHEW 19:12

✦ Where is Jesus's humanity, his human nature here? The idea of a celibate Jesus weighs heavily on his divinity and gives short shrift to his humanity. To assume that Jesus wasn't married is an argument based on silence. If it was typical for a Jewish male to be married, perhaps the Gospel writers would have found a discussion of Jesus's marriage irrelevant or a waste of time. On the other hand, there was a strong minority Jewish movement toward celibacy in the first century. Perhaps Jesus was associated with one of these Jewish groups.

✦ Today we don't assign jobs based on people's ability to sexually reproduce. Yet seeing Christianity in the role of the sexless sexual overseer seems familiar.

7 It is extremely common to have a eunuch oversee the most important things in the Bible. They are in charge of everything valuable that a king or queen might own: jewels, gold, slaves, soldiers, and, most importantly, the sexuality of the king's women.

✦ Paul prefers celibacy to marriage, but he prefers marriage to wanton sexual behavior. This is not quite at odds (but certainly not in agreement) with the authors of 1 Timothy, who think that celibacy is a demonic doctrine and that marrying and childbearing bring salvation. Jesus and Paul seem to offer an alternative to Timothy's vision: celibacy is not only an option, it can be preferential to marriage—a vision that gives everyone, whatever their libido, an honored place in God's kingdom.

Now there was an Ethiopian eunuch, a court official of Candace, queen of the Ethiopians, in charge of her entire treasury.[7] He had come to Jerusalem to worship.

—ACTS 8:27

But if they are not practicing self-control, they should marry. For it is better to marry than seethe with lust.

—1 CORINTHIANS 7:9

✦ The second passage reminds me a little of the old television advertisement in which a woman sings, "I can bring home the bacon. Fry it up in a pan." This woman is superwoman. She is a shrewd shopper; she manages the money; she begins cooking before dawn to prepare meals for everyone; she is able to purchase real estate; she is a farmer; she works out; she sews; she is a philanthropist; she wears the finest clothes, never looking homely; she makes sure her servants are all wearing good warm clothes. On top of all this, she has a great sense of humor and even advises all the men in the city. She doesn't gossip and is a perfect mother. But we are reading someone's fantasy. I'm not sure such a woman (or man, for that matter) has ever existed. What is most valuable to us about this passage is that the woman here isn't confined to domestic work, nor is she submissive or passive. She does many tasks that modern women do today: buys real estate, plants a vineyard, gives wise counsel. The author's idea of the perfect woman is one who is comfortable and capable in all matters of work: business, household, administrative, artisan, and so forth. She would be a real superwoman even today—we would no doubt call her a feminist.

Gender Roles and Cross-Dressing

A woman shall not wear a man's clothing, nor shall a man put on a woman's garment; for whoever does these things is a confusion to the Lord your God.

—DEUTERONOMY 22:5

Who can find a strong woman? Her price is much higher than jewels. The heart of her husband trusts in her, and he does not worry about loss. She does him good, and not harm, all the days of her life. She seeks wool and flax, and works with willing hands. She is like the ships of the merchant, she brings her food from far away. She rises while it is still night and provides food for her household and tasks for her servant-girls. She considers a field and buys it; with the fruit of her hands she plants a vineyard. She girds herself with strength, and makes her arms strong. She perceives that her merchandise is profitable. Her lamp does not go out at night. She puts her hands to the distaff, and her hands hold the spindle. She opens her hand to the poor, and reaches out her hands to the needy. She is not afraid for her household when it snows, for all in her household are clothed in crimson. She makes herself coverings; her clothing is fine linen and purple. Her husband is known in the city gates, taking his seat among the elders of the land. She makes linen garments and sells them; she supplies the merchant with sashes. Strength and dignity are

(continued on page 85)

1 This passage is a good example of the diversity of women's roles in the ancient world. It serves as a model for us today when we think of all the things a woman is capable of doing. Later Christian writings (see Ephesians 5:22–33) do not offer women the same kinds of authority and autonomy that this Proverbs passage gives us.

2 The hierarchical model of the world is set firmly in the early Christian church: Christ, church, male, female. It is also a model that depicts a loving union of the husband and wife. Just as the Hebrew Bible's authors saw God's relationship with Israel through the metaphor of the husband and wife (though it was often a dysfunctional, sometimes abusive relationship), the author of Ephesians's primary message is that the husband and wife should mirror Christ and the church. It is a reverse metaphor, however. The prophets used a metaphor of humans to talk about God; the New Testament authors are using a metaphor of Jesus to talk about humans.

3 The author of Ephesians saw the relationship of Jesus and the church not only as a loving, tender one, but also as an erotic one. The images specifically evoke the physical union of a husband and wife. This trace of eroticism in early church thought never disappeared. You see it especially in analogies between the lovers in Song of Songs to Jesus and the church. Some of the mystics were especially fond of the allegory of sexual intercourse between Jesus the groom and his bride the church.

✦ While this Ephesians passage explains the place of women in an early Christian social structure and portrays submission as a loving act, it is still submission. For some women today it is a difficult concept to accept. Many do not sanction the premise of men's natural superiority over women, and therefore would not accept the Bible's argument that men should rule over women because God made them that way. On the other hand, some women find power in submission. The Bible can be used to legitimize any social position a woman chooses to hold. Proverbs tells her she can be strong, public, and assertive; Ephesians tells her she can be a wife, a mother, and a loving servant to her husband and family. These are all good choices for those who want them. The Bible tells a woman what she *can* be, not what she *must* be.

her clothing, and she laughs at the time to come. She opens her mouth with wisdom, and the teaching of kindness is on her tongue. She looks well to the ways of her household, and does not eat the bread of idleness. Her children rise up and call her happy; her husband too, and he praises her.[1]

—PROVERBS 31:10–28

Wives, be submissive to your husbands as you are to the Lord. For the husband is the head of the wife just as Christ is the head of the church, he is the savior of its body.[2] Just as the church is submissive to Christ, so also wives ought to be, in everything, to their husbands.

—EPHESIANS 5:22–24

✦ The call to be a "good man" in Ephesians is not so easy either. Men are also called to submit themselves to their wives, as Jesus submitted himself to God for the church. A husband must love his wife as he loves his own body.

✦ The author of Colossians believes that being a "good" woman (and a good Christian) means you must submit to the will of your husband. One of my favorite philosophers, Judith Butler, writes that society punishes those who fail to do their gender correctly. We punish them through name calling (dyke, bitch, faggot, fairy), imprisonment (juridical or mental institutions), social stigma, or by denying them certain rights. While religion often sets out standards of civil, social, and virtuous behavior, it is difficult, if not impossible, to differentiate between being morally good and conforming to social expectations. In fact, sometimes it all becomes the same thing. We tend to label those who are social deviates as morally "bad people." According to this verse, a woman who does not obey her husband is a bad person. There is no allowance for his behavior. The verse immediately following this one (3:19) tells husbands to never treat their wives harshly. I would feel much better if that verse preceded this one.

Husbands, love your wives, just as Christ loved the church and gave himself up for her, in order to make her holy by cleansing her with the washing of water by the word, so as to present the church to himself in splendor, without a spot or wrinkle or anything of the kind—yes, so that she may be holy and without blemish. In the same way, husbands should love their wives as they do their own bodies. He who loves his wife loves himself. For no one ever hates his own body, but he nourishes and tenderly cares for it, just as Christ does for the church, because we are members of his body. "For this reason a man will leave his father and mother and be joined to his wife, and the two will become one flesh."[3] This is a great mystery, and I am applying it to Christ and the church. Each of you, however, should love his wife as himself, and a wife should respect her husband.

—EPHESIANS 5:25–33

Wives, be submissive to your husbands, as is fitting in the Lord.

—COLOSSIANS 3:18

1 There is a general rule (it seems to be a custom even before it shows up in Leviticus) in the Hebrew Bible that if a woman's husband dies before she has produced an heir for his estate, it is the obligation of the nearest kin, usually a brother, to have sex with her so that she can produce an heir for her dead husband. In this case, Onan, the second youngest, does not want to provide an heir for his dead older brother. If Tamar doesn't have a son, Onan's own son will inherit all of his father Judah's property. So in a classic case of *coitus interruptus,* Onan pulls out of Tamar before he ejaculates. God is displeased with Onan for this and kills him. Some think that God kills Onan because he wastes his semen. Rather, God's displeasure is more about Onan's disobedience and trickery than it is about masturbation.

✦ This passage is often understood to be about masturbation; in fact, it is where we get the archaic term for masturbation, *onanism*. I don't see that this passage has anything at all to say about masturbation. Some have argued that it is about God's disapproval of nonprocreational sex, but there is no prohibition against masturbation in the Bible.

2 "Covering his feet" could be a subtle euphemism for masturbation. "Feet" is often used in the ancient world as a euphemism for genitals. Some have interpreted "covering his feet" as "relieving himself," which could possibly work here, but the Bible's authors are not usually shy when they talk about urinating. For example, they refer to men as "those who piss against the wall" (e.g., 1 Samuel 25:22; 2 Kings 9:8). Another possibility is that he was defecating. In this passage, masturbation works better because he is in his bed chambers, in private, and the men wait an extremely long time before they bother him. The following verse says that "they waited until they were embarrassed."

3 As she tells us that she is sleeping, we are about to be privy to a sexual fantasy. The woman character of these songs is fantasizing about a visit from her lover.

Masturbation

But since Onan knew that the offspring would not be his, he spilled his semen on the ground whenever he went in to his brother's wife, so that he would not give offspring to his brother.[1] What he did was displeasing in the sight of the Lord, and he put him to death also.

—GENESIS 38:9–10

After he had gone, the servants came. When they saw that the doors of the roof chamber were locked, they thought, "He must be covering his feet in the cool chamber."[2]

—JUDGES 3:24

I slept, but my heart was awake. Listen! my beloved is knocking. "Open to me, my sister, my love, my dove, my perfect one for my head is wet with dew, my locks with the drops of the night."[3] I had put off my garment; how could I

(continued on page 91)

4 The language is delightfully erotic, with lots of double entendres and sexual imagery. The locks of the head dripping with dew suggest moist pubic hair, while *feet* is often a euphemism for genitals in the Bible.

5 This passage is incredibly sexually suggestive with its stark eroticism.

✦ The Song of Songs is an honest-to-goodness celebration of human sex. It doesn't mention God at all, just a deep and carnal attraction between a man and a woman. Many have tried to spiritualize this work, seeing it as a metaphor between God as husband and Israel as his loving bride, or as "spiritual intercourse" between Jesus and his bride the church. We should read this work as an affirmation of lust, love, and sex.

6 God's charge here is that the woman, Jerusalem, melted down the gold and silver gifts from her husband, Yahweh, made phallic images with them, and masturbated.

7 "Defiled herself" is possibly a reference to masturbation, even though such activity for women may not have qualified as "defiling," and certainly men and women alike can "defile" themselves by simply worshiping an idol with no sexual activity implied. Yet, the archaeological find of hundreds of small phallic-shaped images of deities makes the idea of sexual self-defilement with idols easier to imagine.

put it on again? I had bathed my feet; how could I soil them?[4] My beloved thrust his hand into the hole, and I craved him from within my bowels. I arose to open to my beloved, and my hands dripped with myrrh, my fingers with liquid myrrh, upon the handles of the bolt.[5] I opened to my beloved, but my beloved withdrew and was gone.

—SONG OF SONGS 5:2–6

You have also taken your beautiful jewels of my gold and of my silver, which I had given to you, and you made yourself male images and you had sex [committed fornication] with them.[6]

—EZEKIEL 16:17

She whored around with them, with all the great men of Assyria, and with all the men she adored; with all their idols she defiled herself.[7]

—EZEKIEL 23:7

1 Being naked doesn't seem to concern God in Eden—it's the self-realization of who and what we are that seems to be problematic here.

2 Being naked is all about the genitals. This simple statement, that the man and woman took fig leaves and covered their genitals, has forever linked nakedness, sex, and shame. My students always want to know where they got the needle and thread, and who taught them how to sew. The woman's bare breasts are not problematic, and once she covers her genitals she is no longer considered naked.

3 The image of God walking in the garden in the cool of the evening is one of the most compelling images in the Bible. It is an intimate and human portrayal of God. The man and woman are hiding from him and he doesn't know where they are. This isn't the omnipotent and omniscient God we're used to seeing in the Bible.

4 Being naked causes the man to be afraid. Again, the problem doesn't seem to be with his being naked—it's the recognition of the difference between being naked and being covered. In covering their nakedness the first man and woman have chosen to be less vulnerable to God. This passage challenges us to be more accessible to God, with all our flaws hanging right out there.

✦ The Hebrew words *galah ervah* are translated both as "uncovering nakedness" and as being exiled from God's promised land (I translated it as "naked"). There is a play on words here in the creation story. When the man and woman choose not to expose themselves to God, they are choosing to be exiled from God. So, our choices are to translate this passage either figuratively or literally: God wants us to be vulnerable in God's presence, or, God wants us naked.

Nakedness

Then the eyes of both were opened, and they knew that they were naked;[1] and they sewed fig leaves together and made loincloths for themselves.[2] They heard the sound of the Lord God walking in the garden at the time of the evening breeze,[3] and the man and his woman hid themselves from the presence of the Lord God among the trees of the garden. But the Lord God called to the man, and said to him, "Where are you?" He said, "I heard the sound of you in the garden, and I was afraid, because I was naked; and I hid myself." He said, "Who told you that you were naked? Have you eaten from the tree of which I commanded you not to eat?"[4]

—GENESIS 3:7–11

5 Ham, the youngest son of Noah, enters the tent, looks at his father's genitals, and then tells the others. We know that Ham entered the tent, even though the Bible does not explicitly say this, because he tells his two brothers who were "outside the tent." Levitical law says not to "expose the nakedness" of your father. However, the Levitical passage is about incest prohibition—it uses the euphemism of "exposing the nakedness" for sexual intercourse. There isn't a prohibition on looking. The other two actions are probably more troublesome than the first: Ham enters Noah's tent, which is, elsewhere in the Bible, a euphemism for sex, and then he tells his brothers.

6 Shem and Japheth do not look at their father's genitals; instead, they walk backward and cover him without looking at him.

7 What did Ham do? It is not clear why Noah would get so angry at Ham, unless the passage is about something more shameful: sex. The story has strong parallels to the incestuous story of Lot and his daughters (see p. 155).

8 The ark had been with the house of Obed-Edom, and those people had been abundantly blessed, so David decided to move the ark of the covenant to Jerusalem.

9 In verse 14, David put on an ephod, a priestly garment that could be either a kind of apron or a skirt, and leapt and danced. He was ecstatically worshiping God. Probably out of jealousy because all of the girls can see his privates, Michal gets extremely angry with David. The ephod, it seems, didn't conceal David's genitals. Or, perhaps she is seething because she is the daughter of Saul; her brother Jonathan or her own offspring should be king of Israel, not David.

[Noah] drank some of the wine and became drunk, and he lay uncovered in his tent. And Ham, the father of Canaan, saw the nakedness of his father, and told his two brothers outside the tent.[5] Then Shem and Japheth took a garment, laid it on both their shoulders, and walked backwards and covered the nakedness of their father; their faces were turned away, and they did not see their father's nakedness.[6] When Noah awoke from his wine and knew what his youngest son had done to him, he said, "Curse Canaan! He shall be the lowest of slaves to his brothers."[7]

—GENESIS 9:21–25

As the ark of the Lord came into the city of David,[8] Michal daughter of Saul looked out of the window, and saw King David leaping and dancing before the Lord; and she despised him in her heart.[9]

—2 SAMUEL 6:16

10 Michal is sarcastic here; she is chastising David for flaunting his privates in front of all the young handmaidens.

11 David responds that he was dancing naked just for God, not for anyone else. And he also manages to rub it in that God chose him as king over her father.

✦ This passage suggests, as does Genesis 3:7–11, that God may prefer us naked. David justifies dancing naked in public because he was performing for God.

✦ It is also worth noting that the same behavior (ecstatic, half-naked dancing) that can get you arrested in the street can get you praised in a Pentecostal church. There is so much shame connected with sexuality that its connection with the sacred has been all but lost.

David returned to bless his household. But Michal the daughter of Saul came out to meet David, and said, "How the king of Israel honored himself today, uncovering himself today before the eyes of his servants' maids, as any vulgar fellow might shamelessly uncover himself!"[10] David said to Michal, "It was before the Lord, who chose me in place of your father and all his household, to appoint me as prince over Israel, the people of the Lord, that I have danced before the Lord."[11]

—2 SAMUEL 6:20–21

1 This "discharge" is commonly understood to be an abnormal discharge, perhaps attributed to a sexually transmitted disease. Leviticus 15:16–18 specifically addresses "normal" seminal discharge, that is, during wet dreams or intercourse, but this section appears to be directed at diseased discharge. Both Christian and Jewish commentators have referred to verses 2–3 as addressing gonorrheal discharge.

2 There is no judgment against the person or a declaration of sin against God. The person with the discharge is proclaimed unfit to participate in community worship until his discharge stops for a full seven days. Then, on the eighth day, he must take a purity offering to the priest who will declare him clean and fit to participate again in ritual.

3 The main concern here isn't that the penis is discharging; it's that it isn't functioning normally. If the penis is unable to ejaculate, or if it has discharge when it shouldn't, it isn't a whole and working penis, which is essential in ancient Israel (see Deuteronomy 23:1).

✦ The Bible doesn't say anything about sexually transmitted diseases (STDs) as sin. It simply regards them as "uncleanness" that must be remedied (just as women who menstruate are unclean). The shame that accompanies sexually transmitted diseases today often keeps people from going to their doctors or telling their sex partners about the disease. It would help if we could approach STDs as the Israelites did: instead of being shamed into silence and inaction, they recognized that something was wrong and they needed to do the proper things to make sure everything was made normal and safe again. Sexual shame does much more damage than good.

Sexually Transmitted Disease and Genital Abnormality

When any man has a discharge from his member,[1] his discharge makes him ritually unclean.[2] The impurity of his discharge is this: whether his member flows with his discharge, or his member is stopped from discharging, it is uncleanness for him.[3]

—LEVITICUS 15:2–3

4 Wounded or crushed testicles mean no reproduction. Though a penis is present, it malfunctions. The Hebrew word for penis (*shopkah*) derives from a root word meaning "gush" or "pour out." The penis is defined primarily by its ability to gush. A penis that doesn't gush isn't a penis.

5 The absence of a penis is a big problem. Consider this: if God is imagined as male, which God often is in the Bible, and God is considered to be perfect, it is almost impossible for anyone who lives within this worldview to have "flawed masculinity" anywhere near God (females are also considered to be flawed masculinity).

6 Males without a whole and working penis become more like women and thus, according to this line of thought, farther from God.

✦ In our modern ways of thinking we tend to define something and determine its value by its function. Our culture defines and values men by their penis and women by their uterus. For men, we are often obsessed with the size of the penis, the amount of its discharge, and even a man's sperm count. For women, even early Christianity granted her salvation based upon her ability to have babies (1 Timothy 2:15). It is no wonder, then, that today the vasectomy, a simple and safe procedure, is such a stigma for men. The messages have always been that a lack of a full and working penis means you're not a "real" man. And it is no surprise that so many women do not feel like women after a hysterectomy. The message for women is that their worth is through a functioning and productive uterus. We do not need to value ourselves according to how many babies we can produce. The Bible offers alternative options for men and women: the talented and assertive woman in Proverbs 31; David, the dancing and singing lover; and the handsome and devout eunuch, Daniel.

No one whose testicles are wounded[4] or whose penis is cut off[5] shall be admitted to the congregation of the Lord.[6]

—DEUTERONOMY 23:1

1 The stories of children who are born out of illicit unions, incestuous relationships, or adulterous affairs are sometimes told to denigrate a people. For example, the author of this passage is saying that the Moabites and Ammonites are incestuous bastards. We still use the term *bastard* today to denigrate people we don't like, and the label usually has nothing to do with the reality of their parentage.

2 This term "bastard" (*mamzer*) is not exactly as we think of it today. Today, when we talk about bastards we simply mean children born out of wedlock. A *mamzer* in this context is the child of a woman who cannot contract a legally valid marriage to the father of the child (but who can contract a marriage to someone else). A child of adultery (where the woman is married to someone other than the father, for example) is a *mamzer,* and the child of an incestuous relationship is a *mamzer* because the parents cannot marry each other.

3 Some of the post-exilic priests—Ezra, for example—did not recognize the marriages between Israelites and foreigners as legitimate.

✦ The book of Deuteronomy can be particularly harsh on anyone who doesn't "fit." This is only one example of how even a child of questionable heritage is ostracized from the community of worship. This verse has been used (wrongly and unjustly) to vilify interracial unions.

"Illegitimate" Children

Thus both the daughters of Lot became pregnant by their father. The firstborn bore a son, and named him Moab; he is the ancestor of the Moabites to this day. The younger also bore a son and named him Ben-ammi; he is the ancestor of the Ammonites to this day.[1]

—GENESIS 19:36–38

A bastard[2] [*mamzer*] shall not be admitted to the assembly of the Lord. Even to the tenth generation, none of his descendants shall be admitted to the congregation of the Lord.[3]

—DEUTERONOMY 23:3

4 Jerusalem, according to this metaphorical passage, is the illegitimate offspring, the unwanted child, of the Amorites and the Hittites. Ezekiel, particularly in chapter 16, makes an argument that the people of Jerusalem suffered exile because they were not faithful to God. Ezekiel's primary metaphor is of Jerusalem as Mrs. God. Mrs. God fools around on God and fornicates with other gods. It is important for Ezekiel to show that Jerusalem had a flawed beginning—as an unwanted child, she could not be trusted, but God trusted her, loved her, and gave her great beauty and riches regardless of her pedigree. Ezekiel presumes that as an unwanted foreigner, who else would love her? This text also suggests that God loves and cares for all unwanted children.

5 The passage could possibly refer to infanticide, that is, killing a newborn, unwanted baby, but it more likely refers to abandonment. We know that infanticide occurred in the ancient world and still occurs today in some parts of the world, mainly to female children. But there isn't any evidence that the Israelites practiced it. Josephus, a first-century Jewish historian, states that the Israelites did not commit infanticide; it was strictly the practice of foreigners. So it is unlikely that Ezekiel, as a priest, would expect death to happen even if he deemed the baby illegitimate. Thus, the metaphorical baby that Ezekiel describes may not be an example of infanticide but of abandonment. The baby was placed in the field to be picked up by adoptive parents, or by those who sold abandoned babies into slavery or turned them into prostitutes.

✦ Often the Bible's customs are not particularly helpful models for us today. However, the first part of Ezekiel 16 depicts God as a compassionate, caring, and generous adoptive parent to an unwanted child. We should follow God's metaphorical example and attend to the abandoned child who is destined for disease, violence, prostitution, or death. Not every child is lucky enough to have a second chance with excellent parents, like the baby in Ezekiel's allegory. The greater odds are that an unwanted baby will live a life of poverty. Our work should be to reduce the number of unwanted children.

Thus says the Lord God to Jerusalem: Your origin and your birth were in the land of the Canaanites; your father was an Amorite, and your mother a Hittite.[4] As for your birth, on the day you were born your navel cord was not cut, nor were you washed with water to cleanse you, nor rubbed with salt, nor wrapped in cloths. No eye pitied you, to do any of these things for you out of compassion for you; but you were thrown out in the open field, for you were abhorred on the day you were born.[5]

—EZEKIEL 16:3–5

Women's Sexuality

1 This law makes it all too clear that women were property in the Bible. They were primarily something that could be bought, traded, or bartered away. Their sole value was their sexuality. To charge a woman with "nonvirginity" was not only a sexual slander, but it was also a charge against her father that he had cheated the guy; he had sold "damaged goods." If the charge was groundless, the husband who made the false charge had to pay damages and could not (ever) divorce the woman. The assurance of a lasting marriage may sound odd to us and may even seem unwelcome if one of the partners hates the other, but it probably meant relief and security for the woman in a time when women needed the protection and honor of marriage.

2 In our modern world, we might think that the real loser here is the woman. If she is innocent, not only does she have to stay married to a man who hates her, but she must also publicly display proof that she is a virgin. What could this proof be? Most scholars assume that the family would secure the sheets from the wedding bed, which would have the blood from her broken hymen. Blood on the sheet would serve as clear evidence that the woman was a virgin on her wedding night. My students always say that they would keep an extra sheet with blood on it (any blood at all) tucked away for just the occasion—clearly before the time of DNA analysis and paternity suits. Not having a bloody sheet would be foolish and would mean that your daughter would be killed on your doorstep.

✦ I suspect that the law itself and the description of the whole spectacle prevented charges from being brought at all, though this type of honor killing still happens in some parts of the world today (e.g., Egypt, Jordan, and Pakistan). If a woman is raped, her family members may kill her to protect their honor. This biblical punishment is one of the strongest examples of how the Bible does not offer solutions to all modern situations. The Bible guides us in some cases, helps build strong communities in others, but it is a product of a different time and a different culture and doesn't always speak directly to our needs and sensibilities.

◻ Virginity

If any man takes a wife, and goes in to her, and then hates her, and brings charges against her that gives her a bad name, saying, "I took this woman, and when I entered into her, I did not find her virginity," then the father of the young woman and her mother shall take and bring out the woman's virginity to the elders of the city in the gate; and the father of the young woman shall say to the elders, "I gave my daughter to this man and he hates her; and behold he has made shameful charges against her, saying, 'I did not find in your daughter her virginity.' And yet here is my daughter's virginity."[1] And they shall spread the cloth before the elders of the city. Then the elders of that city shall take the man and whip him; and they shall fine him a hundred shekels of silver, and give them to the father of the young woman, because he has brought a bad name upon a virgin of Israel; and she shall be his wife; he may not put her away all his days. But if the thing is true, that virginity was not found in the young woman, then they shall bring out the young woman to the door of her father's house, and the men of her city shall stone her to death with stones, because she has wrought folly in Israel by playing the whore in her father's house; so you shall purge the evil from the midst of you.[2]

—Deuteronomy 22:13–21

✦ From the beginning of his Gospel, Matthew interprets the Hebrew prophets to say that, indeed, Jesus is the Messiah (Hebrew: *meshiach,* God's anointed one). Earlier in a genealogy, Matthew shows us how Jesus is a direct descendant of Abraham, and most importantly (because of messianic prophecy), of David. However, this line to David is through Joseph, not Mary (Matthew 1:16). This is a strong indication that Matthew's focus isn't so much on the *technical* virginity of Mary as it is on Isaiah's words that "a young girl" (Hebrew: *almah*) will have a child. If Matthew intends to say that Jesus was miraculously born to a *technical* virgin, he would not have Jesus's lineage drawn through Joseph. Rather, Matthew is more concerned with showing Jesus's connection to David, so he is looking to Isaiah only to confirm that a young girl (*almah,* not *bethulia* [biological virgin]) will conceive. The Greek doesn't help because, unlike Hebrew, there is no separate word for "biological virgin" (as opposed to a young girl of marrying age). *Parthenos* can mean both.

3 Matthew alludes to Deuteronomy 22:13–21 (see earlier) to show that even though Joseph is a righteous, law-abiding man, he rejects the option for a public trial for nonvirgin brides and chooses to release Mary from any marriage agreement. This could indicate that Joseph is, or at least thinks he is, the father. If he brings a false charge against Mary, he stands to lose a lot of money. But he also doesn't seem to want to marry her (perhaps to protect his own honor) until he has the dream. Matthew's allusion to the Deuteronomy passage and the sexually suspicious women in Jesus's genealogy suggest that people have been talking about how this unmarried young girl has become pregnant. Joseph's dream tells him that he should marry her anyway. Matthew's mention of Tamar, Bathsheba, Rahab, and Ruth (1:1–17) reminds us, and Joseph, that from the wombs of the sexually suspect come the greatest people of all.[4]

4 The dream reiterates that Joseph is of the House of David—again suggesting that Matthew thinks Joseph is the father of Jesus.

Now the birth of Jesus Christ took place in this way. When his mother Mary had been betrothed to Joseph, before they came together she was found having the Holy Spirit *in utero* and her husband Joseph, being a righteous man and unwilling to expose her publicly, resolved to release her from the betrothal secretly.[3] But as he considered this, behold, a messenger of the Lord appeared to him in a dream, saying, "Joseph, son of David,[4] do not fear to take Mary as your wife, for that which is conceived in her is of the Holy Spirit; she will produce a son, and you shall call his name Jesus, for he will save his people from their sins."

(continued on page 113)

5 This does not mean that Joseph didn't have sex with her before the dream. It only states that he doesn't have intercourse with her until after Jesus was born. There is an interesting manuscript variation here. Some documents say "until her son was born"; others say "until her only son was born"; and still others say "firstborn son," implying that there are more to come. The King James Version goes with "firstborn son," and the NRSV translates this verse as "a son."

✦ The theological doctrine of Mary's virginity has put undo pressure on women for many centuries. Rather than the supernatural event of virgin birth, a real source of comfort in Jesus's birth story is that Mary's troubles are common ones for some women today: she is young, she is pregnant, and she doesn't have a husband.

6 In contrast to Matthew, where Mary's first appearance is after she is already pregnant, Luke gives an account of the actual conception of Jesus. In language that echoes the sexual rhetoric of the Hebrew Bible, the angel "comes in" to Mary.

7 Luke is most interested in showing that Jesus's birth is special—Jesus is conceived by the Holy Spirit through a messenger (just as the messengers and God were conflated in the Hebrew Bible). He is destined to be the salvation of Israel. Again, the technicality of virginity isn't Luke's concern; Luke wants us to know, above all, that God impregnates Mary. For Jesus to be without sin, he cannot be conceived by human sperm, which carries original sin.

✦ Mary's virginity and her own immaculate conception only become central in the mid- to late fourth century when the church fathers began to worry about the perfection (sinlessness) of Jesus in light of the taint of original sin.

✦ For modern women, Mary (according to the church fathers) sets an impossible standard: to be a good mother and to remain a virgin. There are words here much more valuable to women today than the idea of virginity and abstinence. Luke's gift to us is an extension of Matthew's presentation of Mary. Not only is she an unwed, pregnant woman, but Luke also stresses the lowliness and poverty of Jesus's origins. There is hope here for women.

All this took place to fulfill what the Lord had spoken by the prophet: "Behold, a young woman [*parthenos*] shall conceive and bear a son, and his name shall be called Emmanuel" (which means "God with us"). When Joseph awoke from sleep, he did as the messenger of the Lord commanded him; he took her as his wife, but did not have sex with her until she had her firstborn son; and he named him Jesus.[5]

—MATTHEW 1:18–25

In the sixth month the messenger Gabriel was sent from God to a city of Galilee named Nazareth, to a virgin betrothed to a man whose name was Joseph, of the house of David; and the virgin's name was Mary. And coming in to her[6] he said, "Hello, honored one, the Lord is with you." But she was very troubled at the saying, and deliberated about what sort of greeting this might be. And the angel said to her, "Do not be afraid, Mary, for you have found favor with God. And behold, you will conceive in your womb and bear a son, and you shall call his name Jesus. He will be great, and will be called the Son of the Most High; and the Lord God will give to him the throne of his father David, and he will reign over the house of Jacob for ever; and of his kingdom there will be no end."[7]

—LUKE 1:26–33

✦ One of the implications of this story is that prostitutes seem to be a part of the landscape in ancient Israel. Visiting them wasn't encouraged, but according to this story, it wasn't forbidden (that is, if the woman does not belong to anyone else).

1 Tamar, Judah's daughter-in-law, has been expecting Judah to give his youngest son, Shelah, to her in marriage as soon as he is old enough. The problem is, she has already married (so to speak) two of Judah's sons and they both have died. Judah is no doubt reluctant to give up his only living son, even though the custom of the land is that he is supposed to.

2 Tamar takes matters into her own hands: she puts a veil over her face and sits by the side of the road waiting for Judah as he travels by on a business trip. He doesn't recognize her because she has covered her face. He thinks she is a prostitute, so he propositions her in typical euphemistic fashion for the Bible, asking how much "to let me come in to you?"

3 The Bible says nothing at all against Judah for visiting a prostitute on a business trip. Perhaps, the assumption is that he is unmarried—so what? Then, the Hebrew word for Tamar here is *zonah,* or whore, which suggests a common streetwalker. Like a good business woman, Tamar makes him leave a security deposit. He leaves his signet, its cord, and his staff. This is overkill; it would amount to leaving your credit card and driver's license with a hooker. Judah appears to be a novice at this, but Tamar seems to know quite a lot. She knows where prostitutes would appear, how much to charge, and how to secure payment.

Prostitution

And when Tamar was told, "Your father-in-law is going up to Timnah to shear his sheep," she took off her widow's garments, and put on a veil, wrapping herself up, and sat at the entrance to Enaim, which is on the road to Timnah; for she saw that Shelah was grown up, and she had not been given to him in marriage.[1] When Judah saw her, he thought her to be a whore, for she had covered her face. He went over to her at the road side, and said, "Come on, let me come in to you," for he did not know that she was his daughter-in-law.[2] She said, "What will you give me, that you may come in to me?" He answered, "I will send you a kid from the flock." And she said, "Will you give me a pledge, till you send it?" He said, "What pledge shall I give you?" She replied, "Your signet and its cord, and your staff that is in your hand." So he gave them to her, and went in to her, and she conceived by him.[3] Then she arose and went away, and taking off her veil she put on the garments of her widowhood. When Judah sent the kid by his friend the Adullamite to receive the pledge from the woman's hand, he could not find her. And he asked the men of the place, "Where is the holy woman who was at Enaim by the wayside?" And they said, "No holy woman has been here." So he returned to Judah, and said, "I have not found her; and

(continued on page 117)

4 When Judah sends an associate to pay for Tamar's services and retrieve his belongings, no one is there. The associate asks around for the priestess—the Hebrew here changes the word from *zonah* (whore) to *qedasha* (holy woman). Either Judah did not tell his friend that he visited a hooker on this trip or this is the way to politely, discreetly, or euphemistically inquire about prostitutes. She is, of course, nowhere to be found. Judah assumes that he has been cheated and doesn't want to be laughed at.

5 Just as he was forgetting about the whole thing, Tamar's pregnancy is discovered and he demands that she be burned, though it is not clear why. When Judah realizes that he is the father of Tamar's child, he declares her more righteous (law-abiding) than he is: she has followed the code that says his family must produce an heir for her, even if she had to trick him into having sex. Tamar bears a son, Perez, whose descendents are David and, eventually, Jesus (see Matthew 1:3–6). This story isn't about following the law no matter what; rather, it reminds us not to make snap judgments about people. If Judah and the others had failed to listen to Tamar's story, there would be no David, and there would be no Jesus.

✦ This story about prostitution, trickery, and righteousness is an excellent reminder to us that, sometimes, those whom society judges as sexually immoral (in this case, Tamar) are the righteous ones. I learn this daily with my students. You can't judge them by what they wear (or don't wear), or by how many visible tattoos and piercings they have. There are enormous hearts and brains beneath the trappings of pseudo-immorality.

also the men of the place said, 'No holy woman has been here.'" And Judah replied, "Let her keep the things as her own, lest we be laughed at; you see, I sent this kid, and you could not find her."[4] About three months later Judah was told, "Tamar your daughter-in-law has played the whore; and moreover she is with child by whoredom." And Judah said, "Bring her out, and let her be burned." As she was being brought out, she sent word to her father-in-law, "By the man to whom these belong, I am with child." And she said, "Acknowledge, I beg you, whose these are, the signet, its cord and the staff." Then Judah acknowledged them and said, "She is more righteous than I, inasmuch as I did not give her to my son Shelah." And he did not lie with her again.[5]

—GENESIS 38:13–26

6 At first glance it's not clear why this verse should go under a section about prostitution. If you look at most English translations of this verse, however, you will see that the Hebrew word *qedasha* (literally, holy woman, i.e., female priest) is translated as "cultic prostitute" and that *qedash* (literally, holy man) becomes "sodomite." In the feminine form, the literal meaning of "female priest" gets turned into "prostitute" because, in the mind of the translators, if you worship the one true God, you must be male to be a priest. If you are female and a priest, you must be worshiping a different god; you must be an idolater, which means you are cheating on God. The translation of "sodomite" is a little trickier. Some argue that homoerotic intercourse was a standard practice in the worship of the Canaanite gods and goddesses. Perhaps this is the case, but the term "sodomite" is quite possibly the ancient masculine equivalent of calling a woman who doesn't fit in a "whore."

7 Verse 18 is an independent rule and should not be read, as most English translations do, as a continuation of the verse on priestesses and priests. The words for prostitute are different. The first is literally "holy woman." The second is "whore." The second law limits what kind of earnings can be used to pay certain tithes in the house of the Lord. Oddly, there is no restriction on *being* a prostitute; she just cannot use the money she earns to make any kind of offering to God. The meaning of "wages of a dog" isn't clear. The NRSV translates this as "wages of a male prostitute," but the Hebrew literally means "dog."

✦ I know I'm jumping through a lot of scholarly hoops, but I want to make this one simple point: many judgments and biases against prostitution and homosexuality are not found in the Hebrew-language text; they are often products that have been imported by translators.

8 The word *abomination* (literally, confusion, mixing) indicates that there is some sort of unwanted mixing of two unlike things going on. For example, bringing "dog" money (a dog was an unsuitable offering) to the house of the Lord, or gentile money, or a priest of a foreign god would all make sense in this line of thinking.

There shall be no woman priest among the daughters of Israel, neither shall there be a priest [of other gods] among the sons of Israel.[6] You shall not bring the hire of a whore, or the wages of a dog, into the house of the Lord your God in payment for any vow;[7] for both of these are a confusion to the Lord your God.[8]

—DEUTERONOMY 23:17–18

✦ Like Genesis 38 (the story of Tamar) this biblical passage does not forbid prostitution nor does it criticize prostitutes.

9 Some argue that the spies have no intention of having sex with Rahab the prostitute, but nearly every sexual euphemism of the Bible shows up in the first three verses of this passage: "come in to," "enter," "lying with." Joshua sends the men to spy out "the entire land," particularly Jericho, yet the first thing they do is go to the prostitute's house. Maybe they think that strangers would blend in there, foreign men may not be so conspicuous. Perhaps they think it might be a good place to gather information.

And Joshua the son of Nun sent two men secretly from Shittim as spies, saying, "Go, view the land, especially Jericho." And they went, and came into the house of a whore whose name was Rahab, and lodged. And it was told the king of Jericho, "Behold, certain men of Israel have come here tonight to search out the land." Then the king of Jericho sent to Rahab, saying, "Bring forth the men that have come in to you, who entered your house; for they have come to search out all the land."[9] But the woman had taken the two men and hidden them; and she said, "True, men came to me, but I did not know where they came from; and when the gate was to be closed, at dark, the men went out; where the men went I do not know; pursue them quickly, for you will overtake them." But she had brought them up to the roof, and hid them with the stalks of flax, which she had laid in order on the roof. So the men chased after them on the way to the Jordan as far as the fords; and as soon as the pursuers had gone out, the gate was shut. Before they lay down, she came up to them on the roof, and said to the men, "I know that the Lord has given you the land, and that the fear of you has fallen upon us, and that all the inhabitants of the land melt away before you. For we have heard how the Lord dried up the water of the Red Sea before you when you came out of Egypt, and what you did to the two kings of the Amorites that were beyond the Jordan, to Sihon and Og, whom you utterly destroyed. And as soon as we heard it, our hearts melted, and there was no courage left in any man, because of you; for the

(continued on page 123)

10 Rahab knows who they are, and in her speech she tells them that everyone is afraid of them and their God. She hides them from the king's men and makes a deal with them: she will not turn them in as spies if they will protect her and all of her family when they destroy Jericho.

11 This simple statement tells us volumes about Rahab. It tells us that, for some reason, she is not loyal to the king; she has a pretty large house that she alone owns (see Joshua 2:3—the king says, "Bring forth the men that have come in to you, who entered your house"); she is shrewd (she hides them first to show that she can be trusted); and most importantly, she has a large family for whom she appears to be the protector and provider. It is not the kind of thing one expects the Bible to say about prostitutes.[5]

12 As a signal to the conquering Israelite army, she hangs a red cord in her window to identify her house. (This won't be the last time that red marks the prostitute's house.) We learn in Joshua 6:28 that Rahab and all of her family are saved as promised. She is brought into the midst of Israel, and the Bible remains silent about her occupation. As far as we know, Rahab remained a prostitute. Later traditions have Rahab married to Joshua and becoming ancestors of Jeremiah and Huldah.

✦ The underlying assumption regarding prostitution appears to be that some men have the option or are even entitled to occasionally visit a prostitute. Though the prostitute herself is a social outcast, she is always present and available to males, even in the Bible. As we will see in the following passages, the Bible speaks negatively about prostitution only when it is associated with worshiping other gods. Does this mean men today are free to visit prostitutes? Remember, we are talking about a foreign culture that existed more than two thousand years ago. Though the Bible doesn't criticize males who visit prostitutes, the men who do seem secretive—ashamed?—about it (remember Judah in Genesis 38). Israel's attitudes about prostitutes and men's sexual freedom that we see in the Bible are not "one size fits all" for modern people.

Lord your God is he who is God in heaven above and on earth beneath.[10] Now then, swear to me by the Lord that as I have dealt kindly with you, you also will deal kindly with my father's house, and give me a sure sign, and save the lives of my father and mother, my brothers and sisters, and all who belong to them, and deliver our lives from death."[11] And the men said to her, "Our life for yours! If you do not tell this business of ours, then we will deal kindly and faithfully with you when the Lord gives us the land." Then she let them down by a rope through the window, for her house was built into the city wall, so that she dwelt in the wall. And she said to them, "Go into the hills, lest the pursuers meet you; and hide yourselves there three days, until the pursuers have returned; then afterward you may go your way." The men said to her, "We will be guiltless with respect to this oath of yours which you have made us swear. Behold, when we come into the land, you shall bind this scarlet cord in the window through which you let us down;[12] and you shall gather into your house your father and mother, your brothers, and all of your father's household. If anyone goes out of the doors of your house into the street, his blood shall be upon his head, and we shall be guiltless; but if a hand is laid upon anyone who is with you in the house, his blood shall be on our head. But if you tell this business of ours, then we shall be guiltless with respect to your oath which you have made us swear." And she said, "According to your words, so be it." Then she sent them away, and they departed; and she bound the scarlet cord in the window.

—JOSHUA 2:1–21

13 Paul uses an image here that he uses again and again: the church community is the body of Christ. Each individual is a limb or a body part of Jesus. Because this reference to "member" comes in the midst of a lengthy teaching on purity, with emphases on food and sex, Paul is being a bit more sexually explicit here, trying to get us to imagine that each of us is Jesus's penis, that whomever we have sex with, we are using Jesus's penis to penetrate that person. This image is validated by Paul's reference to becoming one flesh through intercourse.

✦ It would be difficult, if not impossible, to find a biblical reference that tells men not to visit prostitutes. The closest we get is Paul's warning that whatever we do with our bodies, we are doing with Jesus's body. Unlike the writers of the Hebrew Bible, Paul categorizes visiting prostitutes as a type of sexual perversion. Paul's attitude is a marked change from the ancient attitudes that imply that it is an elite male's right to have access to prostitutes. Paul doesn't buy into the victimless crime idea. His understanding is that what one person does affects the whole community. Sexual immorality in one person pollutes and erodes everyone.

Don't you know that your bodies are members[13] of Christ? Should I therefore take the members of Christ and make them members of a prostitute? Never! Don't you know that whoever is united to a prostitute becomes one body with her? For it is said, "The two shall be one flesh."

—1 CORINTHIANS 6:15–16

1 Blood is one of those things, like water, that is acceptable in just the right amount and in the right place, but might be dangerous in larger quantities or in the wrong place. And menstrual blood is ambiguous at best—on the one hand, it comes out of women's bodies at a regular interval. It's a normal thing.

2 On the other hand, it's blood that is not in the body where it belongs. Around this kind of ambiguity is where we see the most religious concern: rules, taboos, rituals, and remedies. All of these things are attempts to control a seemingly uncontrollable thing. And when you are at the mercy of the world around you, anything uncontrollable is dangerous.

3 This passage does not forbid sex with a menstruating woman, but it does reflect the anxiety that menstruation causes. Almost every religious tradition expresses such anxiety either through outright prohibitions and physical separation or through concerns about setting everything right again.

4 This is the only passage in the Bible that forbids sex with a menstruating woman.

✦ One of the biggest questions about this passage concerning the uncleanness of menstruating women is, does this reflect the "real world," or does it reflect the world where the Israelite priestly class was in charge? Though many assume that the woman was physically separated from her community during her period, the text doesn't say that. It just says that if you come into contact with her, you are contaminated for a short while and have to wash yourself. Yet, how would you know if a woman were menstruating? Did she have to wear a sign? Did the women all bleed at the same time every month?

☐ Menstruation

When a woman has a discharge of blood, which is her normal[1] flow from her body, she shall be in her impurity for seven days, and whoever touches her shall be unclean until the evening. And everything upon which she lies during her impurity shall be unclean; everything also upon which she sits shall be unclean. And whoever touches her bed shall wash his clothes, and bathe himself in water, and be unclean until the evening. And whoever touches anything upon which she sits shall wash his clothes, and bathe himself in water, and be unclean until the evening; whether it is the bed or anything upon which she sits, when he touches it he shall be unclean until the evening.[2] And if any man lies with her, and her impurity is on him, he shall be unclean seven days; and every bed on which he lies shall be unclean.[3]

—LEVITICUS 15:19–24

You shall not approach a woman to uncover her nakedness while she is in her menstrual uncleanness.[4]

—LEVITICUS 18:19

1 The "harm" here is additional harm to the mother beyond miscarriage, for example, if she is injured in a way that causes lasting damage, such as the inability to conceive again or if she dies.

2 This law assumes that the injury to the woman is caused by another man and not by her husband. The assumption here is that the woman is the property of her husband. If the husband is the brawler and accidentally (or intentionally) injures her and causes a miscarriage, there is no fine because he has damaged his own property.

3 If the woman is seriously injured or killed, the husband must be compensated for his loss. The Bible explicitly states "life for life" here but does not say this in the event of only a miscarriage; this implies that the author of this passage does not consider the death of an unborn baby a loss of life since it does not have to be compensated with the loss of another life.

✦ A key debate around abortion is whether the unborn child is a human being or not. The authors of this legal passage do not consider an unborn baby a separate human being.

✦ This passage in Numbers could be an early description of an abortifacient, a menstrual extraction, or an emergency contraception. If a man suspects that his wife is fooling around but has no evidence (or, perhaps she is pregnant and he doesn't think it's his), he can bring her to the priest and they will do the "oath of the bitter water." She is brought to the altar, her hair is loosened (to suggest sexual looseness?), and she must hold the barley offering, a sign of her guilt. Then, the priest takes the dust or ashes from the floor of the altar and mixes it with clean water. Supposedly, if the woman has had sex with a man who is not her husband, all kinds of odd things will happen to her body.

Contraception, Abortion, and Miscarriage

When men brawl, and hurt a pregnant woman, so that she miscarries, and yet no harm follows,[1] the one who caused the miscarriage shall be fined, according as the woman's husband determines; and he shall pay the husband as the judges determine.[2] If any harm follows, then you shall give life for life.[3]

—EXODUS 21:22–23

"Say to the people of Israel: If any man's wife goes astray and transgresses against him, if a man lies with her, and it is hidden from the eyes of her husband, and she is undetected though she has defiled herself, and there is no witness against her, since she was not taken in the act; and if the spirit of jealousy comes upon him, and he is jealous of his wife who has defiled herself; or if the spirit of jealousy comes upon him, and he is jealous of his wife, though she has not defiled herself; then the man shall bring his wife to the priest, and bring the offering required of her, a tenth of an *ephah* of barley meal; he shall pour no oil upon it and put no frankincense on it, for it is a cereal offering of jealousy, a cereal offering of remembrance, as a marker of guilt.

(continued on page 131)

4 The Hebrew here is vague and probably colloquial or euphemistic. For example, her "thigh" will fall away. This word *yarek* is typically translated "thigh," "loins," or "shaft" for men. There are only two places where *yarek* refers to women: Numbers 5 and Song of Songs 7:1, which says "the knob of your thigh is like a jewel." The oath goes on to say that the woman's "belly" will "swell." Again, the meaning here is vague. *Beten* is translated into Latin as *cunnus* (female genitals) and in English as "womb" or "belly." Then, it isn't clear if the belly or womb swells or if the genitals somehow protrude or become distended.

"And the priest shall bring her near, and set her before the Lord. And the priest shall take clean water in an earthen vessel, and take some of the dust [or ash] that is on the floor of the tabernacle and put it into the water. And the priest shall set the woman before the Lord, and loosen the hair of the woman's head, and place in her hands the cereal offering of remembrance, which is the cereal offering of jealousy. And in his hand the priest shall have the water of bitterness that brings the curse. Then the priest shall make her take an oath, saying, 'If no man has lain with you, and if you have not turned aside to uncleanness, while you were under your husband's authority, be free from this water of bitterness that brings the curse. But if you have gone astray, though you are under your husband's authority, and if you have defiled yourself, and some man other than your husband has lain with you,' then let the priest make the woman take the oath, and say to the woman, 'the Lord make you an oath and a curse among your people, when the Lord makes your genitals fall away and your belly swell; may this water that brings the curse pass into your womb and make your belly swell and your genitals [thighs] fall away.'[4] And the woman shall say, 'Amen, Amen.'

"Then the priest shall write these curses in a book, and wash them off into the water of bitterness; and he shall make the woman drink the water of bitterness that brings the curse, and the water that brings the curse shall enter into her and cause bitter pain. And the priest shall take the cereal offering of jealousy out of the woman's hand, and

(continued on page 133)

5 Moreover, if she is innocent, the text doesn't say that none of this will happen but that she will "be cleaned out" and will be able to conceive.

✦ This is what I think is happening here: she is pregnant and the husband suspects that it isn't his, or he simply doesn't want the child. He brings her to the priest to receive an abortifacient or a menstrual extraction. The bitter mixture that the woman is made to drink causes either a miscarriage or menstrual bleeding, that is, the lining of her uterus discharges. All of the results described in Numbers 5 are extremely similar to the symptoms that occur when a woman takes the drug Cytotec or Misopristol, a miscarriage-inducing drug. Misopristol, a bitter drug, causes bleeding, cramping, swelling, and finally the evacuation of the womb. The active chemical in Misopristol is prostaglandin, which occurs naturally in all mammalian fatty tissues but with higher concentrations in the livers of cows and ram seminal vesicles.

✦ Ways of controlling fertility and aborting unwanted babies were no doubt available to the women of ancient Israel. Whether or not the account in Numbers 5 is an example of this is certainly debatable but not out of the question. The better question is, did this ceremony actually happen or was it a ritual that was in place just in case? Is it an example of priestly imaginings of the ideal world or is it descriptive of actual circumstances? Either way, this passage indicates at least a working knowledge of women's reproductive functions and attempts to control them either through the use of chemicals or the fear of using them.[6]

shall wave the cereal offering before the Lord and bring it to the altar; and the priest shall take a handful of the cereal offering, as its memorial portion, and burn it upon the altar, and afterward shall make the woman drink the water. And when he has made her drink the water, then, if she has defiled herself and has acted unfaithfully against her husband, the water that brings the curse shall enter into her and cause bitter pain, and her belly shall swell, and her genitals shall fall away, and the woman shall become a curse among her people. But if the woman has not defiled herself and is clean, then she shall be cleaned out, and shall conceive children.[5]

"This is the law in cases of jealousy, when a wife, though under her husband's authority, goes astray and defiles herself, or when the spirit of jealousy comes upon a man and he is jealous of his wife; then he shall set the woman before the Lord, and the priest shall execute upon her all this law. The man shall be innocent, but the woman shall bear her guilt."

—NUMBERS 5:11–31

✦ This beautiful psalm is in praise of God not only for the act of creation, but also for the complexity of humans. Even though we may be rough, without obvious potential, God sees everything we will be. This verse is typically used by pro-life people (those who are anti-abortion) as "proof" that every fetus is fully human, with an entire scripted life in front of her or him.

6 The word *golem* is translated in some versions as "fetus" or "embryo." This is the only time this word shows up in the Bible, but it occurs several times in the Talmud, where it is translated as "unformed [crude] substance," which is what I've used here. In the writings of Jewish mystics it speaks of the nonphysical potentiality of persons.

7 This is a psalm that acknowledges the wondrous creation of God; it celebrates God's faith in us to become full, authentic human beings; and it delights in knowing that even though we may not have the slightest clue what our lives will be, God does. This celebration of human complexity and the marvels of God should not be reduced to a bumper sticker slogan with an agenda.

You created my kidneys, you did knit me together in my mother's womb. I praise you, for you are awesome and wonderful. Wonderful are your works! You know me right well; my strength was not hidden from you, when I was being made in a hiding place, intricately embroidered in the depths of the earth. Your eyes beheld my unformed substance [*golem*];[6] in your book were written, every one of them, the days that were formed for me, when as yet there was none of them.[7]

—PSALM 139:13–16

✦ This verse is also one used by people who are against abortion. It tells us that if God chooses someone to be a prophet, that person is chosen long before he or she was conceived. This verse doesn't apply to each and every conception, although it would be a wonderful thing if every child could be destined to have the love and security as one who has been consecrated by God to be a prophet.

✦ One problem that arises when we use a verse like Jeremiah 1:5 and the passage in Psalms to condemn abortion is that they are used to judge and to vilify the woman who chooses to have an abortion. Though we cannot (and should not) use the Bible to make absolute declarations about abortion—because the word and the event are never specifically mentioned in the Bible—biblical passages can be effective in many situations that arise before, during, and after an abortion experience. For example, if a woman is concerned about God's steadfastness to us and the limits of God's forgiveness, we might consider Romans 8:38 (nothing separates God from us); Psalm 139:1–3 (God understands our actions); or Matthew 18:21–22 (the unlimited forgiveness of God). Further, in the Bible there are stories of righteous people, people of God who were judged and ostracized by a community of people who could not see that God does move in mysterious ways. In the Bible, women whom society has judged and regarded as sexually suspect are often exactly the women through whom God works: Tamar in Genesis 38; Rahab in Joshua 2; and perhaps even Mary, the mother of Jesus. Imagine how her neighbors talked when, as a young, unmarried woman, Mary became pregnant and claimed that she had never had sex with a man.

Before I formed you in the womb I knew you, and before you were born I separated you out; I designated you a prophet to the nations.

—JEREMIAH 1:5

Destructive Sexuality

1 If this is a narrative of a rape, it is an odd one. Since we have nothing from Dinah to judge, we only know what the narrator tells us: that the prince saw her, he took her, and he lay with her. Both verbs, *took* and *lay,* are biblical euphemisms for sex, though they do not typically mean rape, which would be "took with force." (See this example in my notes on translation.)

2 The description of Shechem's feelings for Dinah doesn't discount rape, but it sure seems unlikely. Without the testimony of Dinah, there is nothing to suggest that she was taken against her will. His response to her is exactly the opposite of Amnon's response to Tamar after he rapes her (2 Samuel 13:2–16). Shechem loves Dinah, but Amnon hates Tamar.

✦ This passage about Shechem's desire for Dinah, and their sexual encounter, is missing a crucial voice: Dinah's. We can never know for sure what happened to her. Shechem "saw her and took her," certainly inappropriate by her customs, but I'm not sure if rape is the right word here. What we can learn from this passage is that the circumstances of sexual encounters are not always as clear as we would like. The lines between consensual sex, reluctant sex, and rape can be fuzzy to everyone but the woman (and often, at the time of sex, the woman herself may not be clear). If we don't have the clear voice of the woman involved, we cannot know into which category a sexual situation might fit.

3 The previous verse, Deuteronomy 22:24, states that if a man and a betrothed woman are discovered having sex in the city, both are to be put to death. The authors assume that if she had yelled out, someone would have heard her, so the sex must have been consensual (thus rape is not the issue). The primary issue in this passage is that the woman's sexuality belongs to someone else. The assumption is that she has been forced to have sex with him (since there are no witnesses and no one could hear her cry out, there is no way to know if it was consensual or not).

Sexual Violence, Rape, and Domestic Violence

Now Dinah the daughter of Leah, whom she had conceived by Jacob, went out to visit the women of the land; and when Shechem the son of Hamor the Hivite, the prince of the land, saw her, he took her and lay with her and humiliated her.[1] And his soul was drawn to Dinah the daughter of Jacob; he loved the young girl and spoke tenderly [from his heart] to her.[2]

—GENESIS 34:1–3

But if in the open country a man meets a young woman who is betrothed, and the man forces her and lies with her, then only the man who lay with her shall die.[3] But to the young woman you shall do nothing; in the young woman there is no offense punishable by death, for this case is like that of a man attacking and murdering his friend; because he came upon her in the open country, and though the

(continued on page 143)

4 This law isn't to protect or give retribution to the woman. Rape is not a sexual offense against the woman; it is an offense against her father, husband, or fiancé—it is a property crime. The whole emphasis on this law is to make sure that the third party (husband or husband-to-be of the woman) is compensated for damages (honor and money). To apply this and other biblical passages about forced sex against women to today's situations makes no sense at all. Even though we often put the rape victim on trial, just as they did in the Bible, it is not justice for the woman. In this passage, the Bible's authors were not interested in justice for the woman (her honor can never be restored); they were concerned with economic compensation for damaged property.

5 If this sounds familiar to you, take a look at Genesis 19, the story of the destruction of Sodom. In both stories, strangers visit a foreign land and are given much hospitality by an old man, are invited in, and are having a delightful time. Then, wicked men (and in this case, the Bible is more clear about the gender of the crowd, as opposed to the mixed-gender crowd in the Sodom story) demand that the visitor be thrown out. The old man offers both his virgin daughter and the concubine of his guest, which is his prerogative as the master of the house. He sees the gang rape of the two women as less "vile a thing" than violence against his guest.

6 The Levite grabs his concubine, pushes her out to the mob, and then—goes to sleep? The mob rapes her all night until dawn breaks.

7 She is able to make it as far as the door where she collapses with her hand just on the threshold. Doesn't her master check on her? Doesn't he hear her out there? He doesn't seem to care what happens to her.

betrothed young woman cried for help there was no one to rescue her. If a man meets a virgin who is not betrothed, and grabs her and lies with her, and they are found, then the man who lay with her shall give to the father of the young woman fifty shekels of silver, and she shall be his woman, because he has violated her; he may not release her all his days.[4]

—Deuteronomy 22:25–29

And the old man said, "Peace be to you; I will care for all your needs; only, do not spend the night in the square." So he brought him into his house, and gave the donkeys straw and water; and they washed their feet, and ate and drank. As they were making their hearts merry, behold, certain men of the city, sons of wickedness, surrounded the house, beating on the door; and they said to the old man, the master of the house, "Bring out the man who came into your house, that we may know him." And the man, the master of the house, went out to them and said to them, "No, my friends, do not act so wickedly; seeing that this man has come into my house, do not do this vile thing. Behold, here are my virgin daughter and his concubine; let me bring them out now. Ravish them and do with them what seems good to you; but against this man do not do so vile a thing."[5] But the men would not listen to him. So the Levite seized his concubine, and put her out to them; and they knew her, and abused her all night until the morning.[6] And as the dawn began to break, they let her go. And as morning appeared, the woman came and fell down at the door of the man's house where her master was, till it was light.[7]

(continued on page 145)

8 He only finds her inadvertently as he is opening the house up for the day. He doesn't check to see if she is okay, hurt, or even alive. Where is his compassion? He says simply, "Get up."

9 She doesn't answer; is she dead? We don't know because he doesn't check. We can only hope she is dead when he takes a knife, cuts her up through to the bone, and sends her parts out to the tribes of Israel.

✦ Often in these stories, the woman is a symbol of Israel. She is forcefully penetrated, abused, and dismembered. Following this passage in Judges 20:20, Israel is violently divided through civil war.

✦ Again, we see that sexual violence against women is of no real consequence in the Bible. Male honor is protected first and foremost. In the Bible men aren't punished specifically for sexually abusing women; the crimes of rape and sexual violence are common metaphors (which suggests that it was a familiar occurrence in the land); and women are blamed for the sexual transgressions of men. These attitudes are partly to blame for our own society's negligence in prosecuting and punishing men for sexual violence. As recently as the last century it was assumed that a husband should have the right to physically discipline his wife. This sentiment reflects biblical attitudes; the Bible does little to correct such thinking. Upshot: the Bible is not a one-size-fits-all modern manual on domestic bliss.

10 Amnon wants "to do" something to Tamar. He could just love her, but his love is a love that requires sexual action. And since Tamar is still a virgin, she belongs to the king. Amnon probably knows that David would let him marry her, but he doesn't want that—he only wants to have sex with her.

11 Amnon's shrewd friend Jon'adab knows exactly what kind of love Amnon has for Tamar. When Amnon tells his friend of his love, Jon'adab gives him advice on how to trap and overpower Tamar.

And her master rose up in the morning, and when he opened the doors of the house and went out to go on his way, behold, there was his concubine lying at the door of the house, with her hands on the threshold. He said to her, "Get up, let's go."[8] But there was no answer. Then he put her upon the donkey; and the man rose up and went away to his home. And when he entered his house, he took a knife, and laying hold of his concubine he cut her up, through the bone, into twelve pieces, and sent her throughout all the territory of Israel.[9]

—JUDGES 19:20–29

And Amnon was so tormented that he made himself ill because of his sister Tamar; for she was a virgin, and it seemed impossible to Amnon to do anything to her.[10] But Amnon had a friend, whose name was Jon'adab, the son of Shim'e-ah, David's brother; and Jon'adab was a very shrewd man. And he said to him, "O son of the king, why are you so haggard morning after morning? Will you not tell me?" Amnon said to him, "I love Tamar, my brother Ab'salom's sister." Jon'adab said to him, "Lie down on your bed, and pretend to be ill; and when your father comes to see you, say to him, 'Let my sister Tamar come and give me bread to eat, and prepare the food in my sight, that I may see it, and eat it from her hand.'"[11] So Amnon lay down, and pretended to be ill; and when the king came to see him, Amnon said to the king, "Pray let my sister Tamar come and make a couple of cakes in my sight, that I may eat from her hand."

(continued on page 147)

12 Tamar resists Amnon not because he is her stepbrother and not because she isn't attracted to him, but because she knows that she belongs to David. Amnon, according to Tamar, needs only to ask for David's permission and he can have her. He cannot wait and he doesn't want to keep her. He only wants sex with her.

13 The Hebrew for "being stronger" is a kind of sexual double entendre. It means both "prevailed over her" and "became hard [rigid]."

14 This is not a big surprise; he had no love for her, merely lust.

15 This is the greater offense. While he takes something that belongs to David without permission, he then sends her away. If he had kept her, married her, and not sent her away, Tamar's shame would have been less. It would be the gentlemanly thing to do. Instead, she is now shamed, will be perceived as damaged goods, and has nowhere to go.

✦ The sex of a rape is not something that comes out of love. It is about power and domination. Once the sexual violence occurs, the façade of romance disappears and hate seeps out. Hate has been there all along, thinly disguised as sexual desire. The Bible's attitudes about rape (the right of some men to have complete sexual power over some women) are by no means unique. These attitudes have surfaced in practically every culture and still do. In fact, only the legislation and social movements of the last forty years have shown any progress in addressing and preventing rape. The first rape crisis centers emerged as recently as 1972. Husbands could legally rape their wives in some states until 1993, and only in 1998 was sexual violence listed as a war crime. The Bible can be a comfort for women who have suffered from sexual violence, but not the passages that deal directly with the topic. Rather, look at passages like Isaiah 61:1, which says, "The spirit of the Lord God is upon me, because the Lord has anointed me; he has sent me to bring good news to the

(continued on page 148)

Then David sent home to Tamar, saying, "Go to your brother Amnon's house, and prepare food for him." So Tamar went to her brother Amnon's house, where he was lying down. And she took dough, and kneaded it, and made cakes in his sight, and baked the cakes. And she took the pan and emptied it out before him, but he refused to eat. And Amnon said, "Send everyone away from me." So everyone went out from him. Then Amnon said to Tamar, "Bring the food into the chamber, that I may eat from your hand." And Tamar took the cakes she had made, and brought them into the chamber to Amnon her brother. But when she brought them near him to eat, he took hold of her, and said to her, "Come, lie with me, my sister." She answered him, "No, my brother, do not force me; for such a thing is not done in Israel; do not senselessly disgrace me. As for me, where could I carry my shame? And as for you, you would be as one of the wicked ones in Israel. Now therefore, I pray you, speak to the king; for he will not withhold me from you."12 But he would not listen to her; and being stronger than she, he forced her, and lay with her.13

Then Amnon hated her with very great hatred; so that the hatred with which he hated her was greater than the love with which he had loved her.14 And Amnon said to her, "Get up and get out." But she said to him, "No, my brother; for this wrong in sending me away is greater than the other which you did to me." But he would not listen to her.15

—2 Samuel 13:2–16

oppressed, to bind up the broken-hearted, to proclaim liberty to the captives and release the prisoners." Or, Luke's story of the Samaritan man who showed excessive compassion and abundant love to a foreigner he had never met. These are good models to show that the Bible's concerns are for those who have been abused and broken.

16 The metaphor that Hosea uses (a marriage to a whore) is an extremely effective one for the prophets. The way they see it, God and Israel are married. If Israel allows the worship of foreign gods, or even economically interacts with foreign countries, she is fooling around on God, her husband. For the prophets, idolatry and adultery are the same. However, in order for this metaphor to work, there are some assumptions about men and women we must accept, and for the most part, we do not accept them anymore. For example, imagine a man today in front of a judge and jury arguing, "But your honor, she cheated on me. That's why I stripped her naked in front of her friends, locked her up in the house, and didn't give her water so that she would die. I'm justified in doing that, right?" It's not a defense that would work. But for the prophets and the audience of the prophet (probably elite males), it made sense. For the woman's wanton sexual behavior, she had it coming. Actually this defense might have worked as recently as the first half of the twentieth century, and it might even still be effective with some juries.

"Plead with your mother, plead—for she is not my woman, and I am not her man—that she put away her whoring from her face, and her adultery from between her breasts; lest I strip her naked and make her as in the day she was born, and make her like a wilderness, and set her like a parched land, and kill her with thirst.[16] Upon her children also I will have no pity, because they are children of whoredom. For their mother has played the whore; she who conceived them has acted shamefully. For she said, 'I will go after my lovers, who give me my bread and my water, my wool and my flax, my oil and my drink.' Therefore I will fence in her way with thorns; and I will build a wall against her, so that she cannot find her paths. She shall pursue her lovers, but not overtake them; and she shall seek them, but shall not find them. Then she shall say, 'I will go and return to my first husband, for it was better with me then than now.' And she did not know that it was I who gave her the grain, the wine, and the oil, and who lavished upon her silver and gold, which they used for Ba'al. Therefore I will take back my grain in its time, and my wine in its season; and I will take away my wool and my flax, which were to cover her nakedness. Now I will expose her lewdness [foolishness] in the sight of her lovers, and no one shall rescue her out of my hand. And I will put an end to all her mirth, her feasts, her new moons, her Sabbaths, and all her appointed feasts. And I will destroy her vines and her fig trees, of which she said, 'These are my payments, which my lovers have given me.' I will make them a forest, and the beasts of the field

(continued on page 151)

17 If you are someone who has been in a situation of domestic violence, the words and actions of the prophet Hosea here probably sound all too familiar. He uses the kids to get to the mother. First he tries to talk to the mother through them; then he turns his contempt toward them. The husband continues a string of abusive threats that are still common to us today: he will isolate her, not allowing her out of the house; he will humiliate her in front of her lovers; he will take away the things he thinks he has given her; and he will destroy all of her possessions.

18 Included in certain patterns of domestic violence is the "honeymoon" phase. After the abuser comes to his (or her) senses, there is a period of remorse or of supposed tenderness. The abuser might say, "Oh honey, remember back when we first married, how wonderful things were? You know I love you. If you would only behave, be good, don't make me hurt you, everything would be just fine."[7] It is a powerful metaphor for Israel and God's relationship, but it is based on what we would today see as an abusive relationship. In order to see the prophets' idea of God's forgiveness for Israel as a loving and romantic act, we have to ignore the domestic abuse that goes on throughout the passage. The irony is that this final romantic expression of steadfast love is often used in modern weddings.

✦ This verse is beautiful in its directness and simplicity. I love that it uses the word *never,* which suggests there is no legitimate excuse for abusing (physically or emotionally) your spouse.

shall devour them. And I will punish her for the feast days of the Ba'als when she burned incense to them and decked herself with her rings and jewelry, and went after her lovers, and forgot me, says the Lord.[17]

"Therefore, behold, I will allure her, and bring her into the wilderness, and speak tenderly to her. And there I will give her her vineyards, and make the Valley of Achor a door of hope. And there she shall answer as in the days of her youth, as at the time when she came out of the land of Egypt. And in that day, says the Lord, you will call me, 'My husband,' and no longer will you call me, 'My Ba'al.' For I will remove the names of the Ba'als from her mouth, and they shall be mentioned by name no more. And I will make for you a promise on that day with the beasts of the field, the birds of the air, and the creeping things of the ground; and I will abolish the bow, the sword, and war from the land; and I will make you lie down in safety. And I will betroth you to me forever; I will betroth you to me in righteousness and in justice, in steadfast love, and in mercy. I will betroth you to me in faithfulness."[18]

—HOSEA 2:2–20

Husbands, love your wives and never treat them harshly.

—COLOSSIANS 3:19

✦ This passage tells slaves to submit to beatings and abuses, sometimes sexual, without a word—to suffer in silence. It was used shamelessly and often from plantation church pulpits in the antebellum United States.

✦ Because it immediately follows the directions for slaves to suffer abuse, and it begins with "in the same way," 1 Peter 3:1 has been interpreted to mean that wives should suffer abusive husbands. It has been used by ministers to counsel women in domestic violence situations to submit to the abuse in silence and to try and stick with their relationships. The author likely did not intend this at all, but many today do believe that the husband has complete authority over his wife and that it is within his rights to exercise punishment in some situations. This, however, goes directly against the command in Colossians 3:1.

19 The identity of the author's (traditionally called John) rival prophet is unknown. "John" is adamant that true believers should not participate in the greater Hellenistic culture; in other words, "no mixing." To do so means eating the food that has been offered to Roman gods and thus results in idolatry. Like Hosea, Ezekiel, and Jeremiah, this idolatry represents adultery and sexual immorality (*porneia*).

20 The offending woman, the whore and adulteress, is made sexually vulnerable to all (see Hosea 2:1–13; Ezekiel 23:25–31). Her children are killed as well.

✦ The book of Revelation personifies the religions of the greater society as a sexually immoral woman. By doing this, the author then justifies her gang rape and the death of her children. Even though it is a symbolic story, effective metaphors both draw on contemporary assumptions about women and influence future attitudes.

Slaves, submit to your masters with all deference, not only those who are kind and gentle but also those who are wicked. For it is to your credit if, being aware of God, you endure pain while suffering unjustly. If you endure when you are beaten for doing wrong, where is the credit in that? But if you endure when you do right and suffer for it, you have God's approval. For to this you have been called, because Christ also suffered for you, leaving you an example, so that you should follow in his steps. "He committed no sin, and no deceit was found in his mouth." When he was abused, he did not return abuse; when he suffered, he did not threaten; but he entrusted himself to the one who judges justly. He himself bore our sins in his body on the cross, so that, free from sins, we might live for righteousness; by his wounds you have been healed.

—1 PETER 2:18–24

Wives, in the same way, submit to your husbands, so that, even if some of them do not obey the word, they may be won over without a word by their wives' conduct.

—1 PETER 3:1

But, I have this against you: you tolerate that woman Jezebel, who calls herself a prophet and teaches and deceives my slaves to practice sexual immorality and to eat food sacrificed to idols.[19] I gave her time to repent, but she refuses to repent of her sexual immorality. Beware, I am throwing her on a bed, and those who commit adultery with her I am throwing into great distress, unless they repent of her doings; and I will strike her children dead.[20]

—REVELATION 2:20–23A

1 Lot's older daughter has just witnessed the fiery destruction of Sodom and Gomorrah; she thinks that there is no other man on earth.

2 I always try to picture how the daughters "made" their father drink wine. A funnel? A threat? The text also says that he was so drunk, he didn't know that he even had sex with her. It is stated in just this way so that none of the blame is placed on Lot for having sex with his daughters. The daughters made him drink, got him drunk, and had sex with him without his knowing. The story is more than likely a figurative one.

3 The point of this story is that the Ammonites and the Moabites, foreigners and sometimes enemies of the Israelites, are incestuous bastards.

✦ Maybe the daughters were seeking revenge on Lot—after all, he had offered them up when the violent mob surrounded his house (see Genesis 19:8).

✦ Sex between fathers and daughters is certainly taboo, though I would feel better if the Bible stated this explicitly, which it doesn't.

Incest

Now Lot went up out of Zoar and settled in the hills with his two daughters, for he was afraid to stay in Zoar; so he lived in a cave with his two daughters. And the firstborn said to the younger, "Our father is old, and there is not a man on earth to come in to us after the manner of all the world.[1] Come, let us make our father drink wine, and we will lie with him, so that we may preserve offspring through our father." So they made their father drink wine that night; and the firstborn went in, and lay with her father; he did not know when she lay down or when she rose.[2] On the next day, the firstborn said to the younger, "Look, I lay last night with my father; let us make him drink wine tonight also; then you go in and lie with him, so that we may preserve offspring through our father." So they made their father drink wine that night also; and the younger rose, and lay with him; and he did not know when she lay down or when she rose. Thus both the daughters of Lot became pregnant by their father. The firstborn bore a son, and named him Moab; he is the ancestor of the Moabites to this day. The younger also bore a son and named him Ben-ammi; he is the ancestor of the Ammonites to this day.[3]

—GENESIS 19:30–38

4 Abraham has told King Abimelech that Sarah is his sister, but Abimelech realizes that Sarah is Abraham's wife and not his sister. In his defense Abraham claims that he was telling the truth. Well, a half-truth: Sarah is his half-sister. This tells us that Abraham (or the author of the story) thinks that marrying a half-sister is harmless; he is much more defensive about telling a lie.

5 Read this passage aloud. It makes the heavy repetition of "the daughter of Laban his mother's brother" much more obvious. In the course of the story, the author repeats this phrase five times. The author wants you to know that Jacob is about to marry his first cousin and no one minds at all. Again, it's about keeping all possessions in the family. Abraham made a big deal about making sure that Isaac married a woman from his own family, and Isaac did likewise with Jacob.

✦ Incest is one of those things that each community decides for itself. In the antebellum South and in many aristocratic, land-dependent cultures, people have preferred to marry within the family so that the land stays within the family. In *Gone with the Wind,* Ashley Wilkes marries his cousin Melanie for precisely that reason. Because it is a product of a foreign culture a long time ago, the Bible's criteria for marriage don't always translate readily to our day and age.

And yet she is indeed my [Abraham's] sister; she is the daughter of my father,[4] but not the daughter of my mother; and she became my wife.

—GENESIS 20:12

And it came to pass, when Jacob saw Rachel the daughter of Laban his mother's brother, and the sheep of Laban his mother's brother,[5] that Jacob went near and rolled the stone from the well's mouth and watered the flock of Laban his mother's brother.

—GENESIS 29:10

6 The language here is odd to us; we want it to say "don't expose the genitals of your father's wife because it's a disgusting thing to do" or "because it is your stepmother's genitals." It says explicitly that your stepmother's sex belongs to your father. We can peek here into the mind-set of the ancient Israelites: you don't expose your stepmother's genitals because she and her genitals are your father's property.

✦ This Levitical passage gives all the rules about incest. What is most notable is what is not included: there is no restriction against a man having sex with his daughter. This could be because it was so obvious a no-no that there was no need to state it, or, perhaps, because an unbetrothed daughter was the property of her father and he could have full sexual access to her if he chose.

✦ Again, some of the Bible's stories have not been helpful (and are often harmful) for women who have suffered from incestuous sexual abuse. The Bible does offer passages about compassionate parents and about brothers who love and protect their sisters. But all in all, it is best to remember that much of the Bible is a history of a people. Much of it is not overtly concerned with the care and comfort of women. And often, biblical women symbolize Israel herself. She was invaded, torn apart, and exiled. The Bible's authors were showing that bad things happened to Israel because she was a bad woman and deserved them. This may be an effective metaphor for those contemporary with the prophets but is not helpful for modern women who have been sexually abused and are in need of comfort.

Do not uncover the genitals of your father, or the genitals of your mother: she is your mother; do not expose her genitals. Do not expose the genitals of your father's wife: it is your father's genitals.[6] Do not expose the genitals of your sister, the daughter of your father, or daughter of your mother, whether born at home, or born abroad. Do not expose the genitals of your son's daughter, or of your daughter's daughter: for theirs are your own genitals. Do not expose the genitals of your father's wife's daughter, begotten of your father, she is your sister. Do not expose the genitals of your father's sister: she is your father's near relative. Do not expose the genitals of your mother's sister: for she is your mother's near relative. Do not expose the genitals of your father's brother, do not approach his wife: she is your aunt. Do not expose the genitals of your daughter-in-law: she is your son's wife. Do not expose the genitals of your brother's wife: it is your brother's genitals. Do not expose the genitals of a woman and her daughter, neither shall you take her son's daughter, or her daughter's daughter, to expose her genitals; they are her near relatives: it is wickedness. Neither shall you take your wife's sister, just for spite, to expose her genitals, while both are living.

—LEVITICUS 18:7–18

1 This is a specific commandment for women: do not have sex with animals. Most of the commandments are meant for men only—for example, do not lie with a man as with a woman, and all of the laws about incest. But this one specifically singles out women. This could mean that women were prone to having intercourse with animals, but I doubt it. The threat of women having sex with animals is about the mixing of unlike things. Genesis 6:2 and 6:4 tell us that the sons of God had sex with human women. This suggests to me that in the ancient imagination, the women have to be protected from all sorts of sexual threats. Having intercourse with the divinity (as in Genesis 6) and having sex with animals is an equal threat to the priests: both the divine and animals belong to the world of chaos, the uncontrollable, which threatens certain death for them.

2 This word *toevah* (mixing, confusion, abomination) is the big hint that sex with animals isn't considered so much a sexual sin as something that threatens the stability and security of the whole community. Animals and God belong to the realm of chaos, the uncontrollable. When chaos rules, civilization dies.

Bestiality

You shall not have sexual relations with any animal and defile yourself with it, nor shall any woman give herself to an animal to have sexual relations with it:[1] it is confusion [abomination].[2]

—LEVITICUS 18:23

3 This seems not only incredibly harsh, but also odd and senseless. Does killing the animal set an example to all the other animals? Does it reflect a mentality of blaming the victim? No, it signifies that bestiality isn't primarily punished as a sex offense but as a crime against the so-called natural order of things. If these two different species mix, all of nature could be mixed, the world would be in complete confusion, and civilization would be in ruins. Killing both participants tidies everything up; it puts everything back in its proper place.

✦ What I call the "ick factor" is huge in this passage on having sex with animals. What we must remember, however, is that this law is part of the laws about not mixing unlike things together. For the Israelites, combining two types of clothing material into a single garment would be in the same category as having intercourse with a goat. Today we have managed to put sexual weirdness and food weirdness into separate moral categories. Sexual weirdness has taken on a far greater degree of morality (along with the ick factor); we consider it as both sin and criminal behavior. We still have some of the ick factor in the United States regarding certain foods—eating dogs, for example—but it does not belong to the realm of sin or of criminal behavior. The upshot of this is that we think the Bible is our source of rules about sex. The truth is, we pick and choose rules from the Bible depending on which ones agree with already-held societal beliefs about sexual right and wrong.

If a man has sexual relations with an animal, he shall be put to death; and you shall kill the animal.[3]

—LEVITICUS 20:15

Sexual Joy and Delight

1 The image of Sarah standing just inside the tent listening to this conversation and laughing at the messengers is one of my favorites in the Bible. What I find most delightful here is that Sarah views sex with her husband as pleasurable. Sometimes we think that because a woman's sexuality was considered property in the ancient world, sex was just another duty that had to be performed. Sarah clearly enjoyed Abraham.

2 The verb here that has been translated as "walk" does not show up anyplace else in the Bible. Some English versions follow the Septuagint (the Greek translation of the Hebrew Bible) and translate it as "meditate." I have heard it suggested that perhaps Isaac was going out to relieve himself.

3 Isaac is looking down (at what?); he looks up and sees Rebekah. At the same time, she sees Isaac (perhaps more than she expected) and her reaction is extreme: she falls off her camel.

✦ This is a playful imagining of this story. Since the Hebrew is unclear and translators have no idea what to make of it, a playfully sexual reading here works as well as any. This translation also maintains the lightheartedness of the name *Isaac* (laughter).

4 In the Hebrew, this is a fun play on words. Isaac's name means "laughter" or "fooling around." In other words, Isaac is isaacing. We're not sure what Isaac and Rebekah are doing, but it is such that when Abimelech sees them, he knows that they are husband and wife, not brother and sister (which is what Isaac had told him earlier). Even in a possibly dangerous foreign land Isaac and Rebekah take the time to fool around with each other.

5 This combination of kissing, crying out, and weeping occurs several times in the Bible, but it is usually about grieving a loss. Here, though, there is a sense of ultimate relief. Jacob has found his beloved.

✦ If you are lucky enough to have already met the one you love, you probably recognize Jacob's reaction to Rachel.

Sexual Joy and Delight

Then one said, "I will definitely return to you at the right time, and your wife Sarah shall have a son." And Sarah was listening at the tent entrance behind him. Now Abraham and Sarah were old, advanced in age; Sarah was no longer able to have children. So Sarah laughed to herself, saying, "After I have grown old, and my husband is old, shall I have pleasure?"[1]

—Genesis 18:10–12

Isaac went out in the evening to walk[2] in the field; and looking up, he saw camels coming. And Rebekah looked up, and when she saw Isaac, she fell off her camel.[3]

—Genesis 24:63–64

When Isaac had been there a long time, King Abimelech of the Philistines looked out of a window and saw him fooling around with his wife Rebekah.[4]

—Genesis 26:8

Then Jacob kissed Rachel, cried out, and wept.[5]

—Genesis 29:11

6 This is one of the most-often quoted lines of pure love and delight for a beloved. I always get stuck, however, on the shift from "him" to "your." This is evidence that the poem/song has been chopped up and spliced together in odd ways. As you read through Song of Songs there is constant shifting between a male and female voice and from a third- to second-person voice.

✦ The entire collection of poems is extraordinary for the Bible. It doesn't mention God at all, it never says that the lovers are married, and its thinly veiled allusions to purely physical lovemaking are often graphic.

7 Not only does this analogy suggest that her young man stands out among his peers, it makes special reference to his "fruit." We should imagine the fullness and the temptation of his "hanging fruit." The metaphors of fruit, vegetables, seeds, and sowing for sex are abundant in the ancient Near East, the Bible is fraught with them, and Song of Songs holds at least thirty-eight references to fruit, blossoms, and trees. The blossoms connote images of nipples and of the clitoris; the images of tree trunks, beams, and rafters should remind us of a hard, erect penis. Throughout the song, we see the connections between the fertility of the land, the fertile woman, sowing seeds, and bearing fruit.

8 Again, a switch from "he" to "you." He brings her to the wine house—this is probably a place where the wine is stored to age. Maybe it's the equivalent of sneaking off to the barn if you grew up on a farm. The verse suggests that they have had so much sex, she needs food to sustain her energy.

Let him kiss me with the kisses of his mouth. For your love is better than wine.[6]

—SONG OF SONGS 1:2

As an apple tree among the trees of the wood, so is my beloved among young men. With great delight I sat in his shadow, and his fruit was sweet to my taste.[7] He brought me to the wine house, and his intention toward me was love. Sustain me with raisin cakes, refresh me with apples; for I am faint with love.[8] O that his left hand were under my head, and that his right hand embraced me!

—SONG OF SONGS 2:3–6

9 If you have ever been in love, or at least in the throes of a mighty lust, you know its effects can feel a lot like being drunk. As with inebriation, you cannot focus your thoughts, you don't hear what others are saying, and you may even slur your words.

10 Smell is probably the most powerful sense of all, especially when the senses become sharpened with a ravenous sexual appetite. The Song of Songs uses an extraordinary amount of descriptions of fragrances.

11 Water is a highly erotic image here. The speaker has compared his lover to a garden (a lush, abundantly full, and ripe garden). When she is sexually aroused her waters flow like a stream out of Lebanon.

12 She commands the winds to carry the aroma of her sex to her lover, to bring him to her so that he may "eat of her fruit." This is one of several references to oral sex in Song of Songs.

How sweet is your love, my beloved, my bride! how much better is your love than wine,[9] and the smell[10] of your oils than any spice! Your lips distill nectar, my bride; honey and milk are under your tongue; the scent of your garments is like the scent of Lebanon. A garden locked is my sister, my bride, a garden locked, a fountain sealed. Your channel is an orchard of pomegranates with all choicest fruits, henna with nard, nard and saffron, calamus and cinnamon, with all trees of frankincense, myrrh and aloes, with all chief spices—a garden fountain, a well of living water, and flowing streams from Lebanon.[11] Awake, north wind, and come, south wind! Blow upon my garden that its fragrance may be wafted abroad. Let my beloved come to his garden, and eat its choicest fruits.[12]

—SONG OF SONGS 4:10–16

Notes

1. Ironically, when I was an undergraduate at the University of Tennessee, I discovered that my chair in the religious studies department, Dr. Charles Reynolds, was arrested that night as one of the anti-war protestors.
2. According to the report of the Special Rapporteur submitted to the 58th session of the U.N. Commission on Human Rights (2002).
3. For more on the homoeroticism in this passage, see Bernadette Brooten's *Love Between Women.*
4. See Jane Schaberg's *The Illegitimacy of Jesus* for more information on Matthew's understanding of Mary's virginity.
5. For more on the character of Rahab, see Phyllis Bird's "The Harlot as Heroine: Narrative Art and Social Presupposition in Three Old Testament Texts." *Semeia* 46 (1989): 119–39.
6. There are several articles devoted to Numbers 5:11–31 in the book edited by Alice Bach, *Women in the Hebrew Bible,* pp. 461–522.
7. Renita Weems's *Battered Love* is the source for much of this material.

Suggestions for Further Reading

Aslan, Reza. *No God but God: The Origins, Evolution, and Future of Islam.* New York: Random House, 2005.

Bach, Alice, ed. *Women in the Hebrew Bible: A Reader.* New York: Routledge Press, 1999.

Brenner, Athalya. *The Intercourse of Knowledge: On Gendering Desire and "Sexuality" in the Hebrew Bible*. Biblical Interpretation Series 26. Leiden, Netherlands: Brill, 1997.

Brooten, Bernadette. *Love Between Women: Early Christian Responses to Female Homoeroticism*. Chicago: University of Chicago Press, 1996.

Camp, Claudia. *Wise, Strange and Holy: The Strange Woman and the Making of the Bible*. Sheffield, UK: Sheffield Academic Press, 2000.

Countryman, L. William. *Dirt, Greed, and Sex: Sexual Ethics in the New Testament and Their Implications for Today*. Philadelphia: Fortress Press, 1990.

Eilberg-Schwartz, Howard. *God's Phallus and Other Problems for Men and Monotheism.* Boston: Beacon Press, 1994.

Exum, J. Cheryl. *Plotted, Shot, and Painted: Cultural Representations of Biblical Women.* Sheffield, UK: Sheffield Academic Press, 1996.

Galambush, Julie. *Jerusalem in the Book of Ezekiel: The City as Yahweh's Wife.* Atlanta, GA:Scholars Press, 1992.

Hosseini, Khaled. *The Kite Runner.* New York: Riverhead Books, 2003.

Kamionkowski, S. Tamar. *Gender Reversal and Cosmic Chaos: A Study on the Book of Ezekiel*. Sheffield, UK: Sheffield Academic Press, 2002.

King, Karen. *Gospel of Mary of Magdala:Jesus and the First Woman Apostle.* Santa Rosa, CA: Polebridge Press, 2003.

Levine, Amy-Jill. *The Misunderstood Jew: The Church and the Scandal of the Jewish Jesus*. San Francisco: HarperSanFrancisco, 2007.

Martin, Dale. *Sex and the Single Savior: Gender and Sexuality in Biblical Interpretation*. Louisville, KY: Westminster John Knox Press, 2006.

Newsome, Carol, and Sharon Ringe, eds. *Women's Bible Commentary.* Rev. ed. Louisville, KY: Westminster John Knox Press, 1998.

Russell, Letty, ed. *Feminist Interpretation of the Bible*. Philadelphia: Westminster, 1985.

Schaberg, Jane. *The Illegitimacy of Jesus: A Feminist Theological Interpretation of the Infancy Narratives.* San Francisco: HarperCollins, 1987.

———. *The Resurrection of Mary Magdalene: Legends, Apocrypha, and the Christian Testament.* New York: Continuum Press, 2002.

Streete, Gail Corrington. *The Strange Woman: Power and Sex in the Bible.* Louisville, KY: Westminster John Knox Press, 1997.

Trible, Phyllis. *Texts of Terror: Literary-Feminist Readings of Biblical Narrative.* Philadelphia: Fortress Press, 1984.

Weems, Renita J. *Battered Love: Marriage, Sex, and Violence in the Hebrew Prophets.* Philadelphia: Fortress Press, 1995.

Sacred Texts—cont.

GNOSTICISM

The Gospel of Philip: Annotated & Explained
Translation & Annotation by Andrew Phillip Smith; Foreword by Stevan Davies
Reveals otherwise unrecorded sayings of Jesus and fragments of Gnostic mythology.
5½ x 8½, 160 pp, Quality PB, 978-1-59473-111-2 **$16.99**

The Gospel of Thomas: Annotated & Explained
Translation & Annotation by Stevan Davies Sheds new light on the origins of Christianity and portrays Jesus as a wisdom-loving sage. 5½ x 8½, 192 pp, Quality PB, 978-1-893361-45-4 **$16.99**

The Secret Book of John: The Gnostic Gospel—Annotated & Explained
Translation & Annotation by Stevan Davies The most significant and influential text of the ancient Gnostic religion. 5½ x 8½, 208 pp, Quality PB, 978-1-59473-082-5 **$16.99**

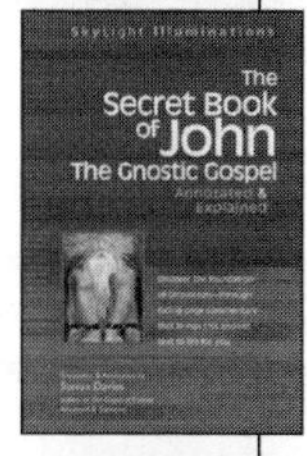

JUDAISM

The Divine Feminine in Biblical Wisdom Literature
Selections Annotated & Explained
Translation & Annotation by Rabbi Rami Shapiro; Foreword by Rev. Cynthia Bourgeault, PhD
Uses the Hebrew books of Psalms, Proverbs, Song of Songs, Ecclesiastes and Job, Wisdom literature and the Wisdom of Solomon to clarify who Wisdom is.
5½ x 8½, 240 pp, Quality PB, 978-1-59473-109-9 **$16.99**

Ethics of the Sages: *Pirke Avot*—Annotated & Explained
Translation & Annotation by Rabbi Rami Shapiro Clarifies the ethical teachings of the early Rabbis. 5½ x 8½, 192 pp, Quality PB, 978-1-59473-207-2 **$16.99**

Hasidic Tales: Annotated & Explained
Translation & Annotation by Rabbi Rami Shapiro
Introduces the legendary tales of the impassioned Hasidic rabbis, presenting them as stories rather than as parables. 5½ x 8½, 240 pp, Quality PB, 978-1-893361-86-7 **$16.95**

The Hebrew Prophets: Selections Annotated & Explained
Translation & Annotation by Rabbi Rami Shapiro; Foreword by Zalman M. Schachter-Shalomi
Focuses on the central themes covered by all the Hebrew prophets.
5½ x 8½, 224 pp, Quality PB, 978-1-59473-037-5 **$16.99**

Zohar: Annotated & Explained *Translation & Annotation by Daniel C. Matt*
The best-selling author of *The Essential Kabbalah* brings together in one place the most important teachings of the Zohar, the canonical text of Jewish mystical tradition.
5½ x 8½, 176 pp, Quality PB, 978-1-893361-51-5 **$15.99**

EASTERN RELIGIONS

Bhagavad Gita: Annotated & Explained *Translation by Shri Purohit Swami*
Annotation by Kendra Crossen Burroughs Explains references and philosophical terms, shares the interpretations of famous spiritual leaders and scholars, and more.
5½ x 8½, 192 pp, Quality PB, 978-1-893361-28-7 **$16.95**

Dhammapada: Annotated & Explained *Translation by Max Müller and revised by Jack Maguire; Annotation by Jack Maguire* Contains all of Buddhism's key teachings.
5½ x 8½, 160 pp, b/w photos, Quality PB, 978-1-893361-42-3 **$14.95**

Rumi and Islam: Selections from His Stories, Poems, and Discourses—Annotated & Explained *Translation & Annotation by Ibrahim Gamard*
Focuses on Rumi's place within the Sufi tradition of Islam, providing insight into the mystical side of the religion. 5½ x 8½, 240 pp, Quality PB, 978-1-59473-002-3 **$15.99**

Selections from the Gospel of Sri Ramakrishna: Annotated & Explained
Translation by Swami Nikhilananda; Annotation by Kendra Crossen Burroughs
Introduces the fascinating world of the Indian mystic and the universal appeal of his message. 5½ x 8½, 240 pp, b/w photos, Quality PB, 978-1-893361-46-1 **$16.95**

Tao Te Ching: Annotated & Explained *Translation & Annotation by Derek Lin; Foreword by Lama Surya Das* Introduces an Eastern classic in an accessible, poetic and completely original way. 5½ x 8½, 192 pp, Quality PB, 978-1-59473-204-1 **$16.99**

About SKYLIGHT PATHS Publishing

SkyLight Paths Publishing is creating a place where people of different spiritual traditions come together for challenge and inspiration, a place where we can help each other understand the mystery that lies at the heart of our existence.

Through spirituality, our religious beliefs are increasingly becoming a part of our lives—rather than *apart* from our lives. While many of us may be more interested than ever in spiritual growth, we may be less firmly planted in traditional religion. Yet, we do want to deepen our relationship to the sacred, to learn from our own as well as from other faith traditions, and to practice in new ways.

SkyLight Paths sees both believers and seekers as a community that increasingly transcends traditional boundaries of religion and denomination—people wanting to learn from each other, *walking together, finding the way.*

For your information and convenience, at the back of this book we have provided a list of other SkyLight Paths books you might find interesting and useful. They cover the following subjects:

Buddhism / Zen
Catholicism
Children's Books
Christianity
Comparative Religion
Current Events
Earth-Based Spirituality
Global Spiritual Perspectives
Gnosticism
Hinduism / Vedanta
Inspiration
Islam / Sufism
Judaism / Kabbalah / Enneagram
Meditation
Midrash Fiction
Monasticism
Mysticism
Poetry
Prayer
Religious Etiquette
Retirement
Spiritual Biography
Spiritual Direction
Spirituality
Women's Interest
Worship

Or phone, fax, mail or e-mail to: SKYLIGHT PATHS **Publishing**
Sunset Farm Offices, Route 4 • P.O. Box 237 • Woodstock, Vermont 05091
Tel: (802) 457-4000 • Fax: (802) 457-4004 • www.skylightpaths.com
Credit card orders: (800) 962-4544 (8:30AM–5:30PM ET Monday–Friday)